FOOD & WINE

BEST OF THE BEST

FOOD & WINE
BOOKS

FOOD & WINE BEST OF THE BEST VOL. 17
EXECUTIVE EDITOR **Kate Heddings**
EDITOR **Susan Choung**
DESIGN DIRECTOR **Patricia Sanchez**
ASSOCIATE ART DIRECTOR **Jooyoung Hsu**
DESIGN CONCEPT **Courtney Waddell Eckersley**
FEATURES EDITOR **Yaran Noti**
RECIPE TESTER **Sue Li**
SENIOR WINE EDITOR **Megan Krigbaum**
COPY EDITOR **Lisa Leventer**
SENIOR PRODUCTION MANAGER **Amelia Grohman**
PRODUCTION ASSOCIATE **Pamela Brandt**
ASSOCIATE PHOTO EDITOR **James Owens**
EDITORIAL ASSISTANT **Sarah Kraut**
RESEARCHER **Michelle Loayza**

FOOD & WINE MAGAZINE
SVP / EDITOR IN CHIEF **Dana Cowin**
EXECUTIVE MANAGING EDITOR **Mary Ellen Ward**
EXECUTIVE EDITOR **Pamela Kaufman**
EXECUTIVE FOOD EDITOR **Tina Ujlaki**
EXECUTIVE WINE EDITOR **Ray Isle**
DEPUTY EDITOR **Christine Quinlan**

Copyright © 2014 and published by Time Inc. Affluent
Media Group, 1120 Avenue of the Americas, New York,
New York 10036

FOOD & WINE is a trademark of Time Inc. Affluent Media
Group, registered in the U.S. and other countries.

ISBN 10: 1-932624-67-8
ISBN 13: 978-1-932624-67-0
ISSN 1524-2862

Manufactured in the United States of America

TIME INC. AFFLUENT MEDIA GROUP
CHIEF MARKETING OFFICER / PRESIDENT, DIGITAL MEDIA **Mark V. Stanich**
VP, FINANCE **Keith Strohmeier**
VP, BOOKS & PRODUCTS / PUBLISHER **Marshall Corey**
DIRECTOR, BOOK PROGRAMS **Bruce Spanier**
SENIOR MARKETING MANAGER, BRANDED BOOKS **Eric Lucie**
DIRECTOR OF FULFILLMENT & PREMIUM VALUE **Philip Black**
DIRECTOR OF FINANCE **Thomas Noonan**
ASSOCIATE BUSINESS MANAGER **Desiree Flaherty**
SENIOR MANAGER, CONTRACTS & RIGHTS **Jeniqua Moore**

TIME HOME ENTERTAINMENT, INC.
SENIOR PRODUCTION MANAGER **Susan Chodakiewicz**

TIME INC.
CHIEF EXECUTIVE OFFICER **Joseph Ripp**
CHIEF CONTENT OFFICER **Norman Pearlstine**
EXECUTIVE VICE PRESIDENT **Evelyn Webster**
EXECUTIVE VICE PRESIDENT, CHIEF FINANCIAL OFFICER **Jeff Bairstow**
EXECUTIVE VICE PRESIDENTS **Lynne Biggar, Colin Bodell,**
    Teri Everett, Mark Ford, Greg Giangrande,
    Lawrence A. Jacobs, Todd Larsen, Evelyn Webster

FRONT & BACK COVERS
PHOTOGRAPHER **Seth Smoot**
FOOD STYLIST **Kendra Smoot**
PROP STYLIST **Christopher Barsch**

BEST OF THE BEST

The Best Recipes from the
25 Best Cookbooks of the Year

FOOD&WINE
Time Inc. Affluent Media Group

CONTENTS

Recipe titles in **bold** are brand-new dishes appearing exclusively in *Best of the Best.*

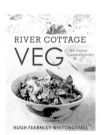

continued on next page

CONTENTS *continued*

Recipe titles in **bold** are brand-new dishes appearing exclusively in *Best of the Best*.

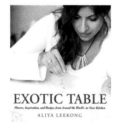

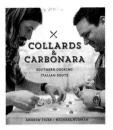

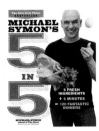
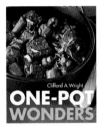

RECIPES

Starters & Soups

Salads

Pasta & Grains

Fish & Shellfish

Poultry

CRUSTLESS BROCCOLI
& CHEDDAR QUICHE, P.54

FOREWORD

HERE at *Food & Wine*, we love spotting trends, and we found some extraordinary ones after reviewing nearly 100 new cookbooks for this year's *Best of the Best*. The first trend that caught our eye: the rise of mash-up cuisines. You can see it right there in titles like *Collards & Carbonara*–chefs are creating new flavors culled from cooking traditions that are oceans apart. In *Smoke & Pickles*, Edward Lee introduces Korean–Southern American cooking; one recipe to try is his squid and bacon salad with a zingy ginger-apple relish (page 138).

We also found that star chefs are solving the weeknight dinner problem. *Michael Symon's 5 in 5* delivers on a basic promise: superfast five-ingredient dinners (try his spicy chicken diablo on page 224). And Curtis Stone organizes recipes by day of the week in *What's for Dinner?*, smartly eliminating the need to waste time even thinking about what to make on any given night.

Finally, the trend that just keeps growing: vegetables. This year, we're using every part of them thanks to Tara Duggan's *Root-to-Stalk Cooking* (we adore her cheesy beet greens strata on page 90), and we're learning more about vegetables than we ever knew before from Deborah Madison's *Vegetable Literacy*.

The amazing recipes throughout this collection–the 114 best of the year–hit on even more exciting trends; we hope you enjoy discovering every last one of them.

Dana Cowin
Editor in Chief
FOOD & WINE

Kate Heddings
Executive Editor
FOOD & WINE Cookbooks

BAKED CLAMS, P.14

THE GRAMERCY TAVERN COOKBOOK

BY **MICHAEL ANTHONY** WITH **DOROTHY KALINS**

HERE'S a look inside the kitchen of one of the most influential New York City restaurants of the past two decades. In this expansive cookbook, chef Michael Anthony explains how his restaurant works day-to-day, profiles his staff and discourses on the importance of good pork and the value of cooking school. But the best parts are the recipes, which illustrate Anthony's finesse. Like the baked clams (pictured at left): To add sweetness, Anthony finely chops scallops and mixes them into the clam filling. The gorgeously photographed food might seem intimidating, but Anthony is reassuring: "Don't worry if your dishes don't look exactly like our photographs. The ingredients themselves are beautiful enough."

Published by Clarkson Potter, $50

BAKED CLAMS

Makes **20 clams**

- 1 **cup white wine**
- 1 **shallot, sliced, plus ¾ cup minced shallots**
- 3 **garlic cloves, smashed, plus 2 tablespoons minced garlic**
- ⅓ **cup finely chopped flat-leaf parsley, plus a few flat-leaf parsley stems**
- 20 **large cherrystone clams, cleaned**
- ¼ **cup olive oil**
- 4 **tablespoons (½ stick) unsalted butter**
- 1¼ **cups minced onions**
- 1¼ **cups minced leeks (white parts)**
- 1½ **tablespoons peeled and minced ginger**
- 2 **teaspoons thyme leaves**

Salt and pepper

- 1¾ **cups panko or dried bread crumbs**
- 7 **ounces sea scallops, cut into small pieces**
- 1 **tablespoon fresh lemon juice**
- 5 **cups rock salt**
- 1 **lemon, cut into 8 wedges**

Editor's Wine Choice
Fragrant, citrusy white: 2012
Birichino Malvasia Bianca

My wife, Mindy, grew up eating classic baked clams on the East End of Long Island. I wanted to tap into her nostalgic feelings for summertime and the beach and amplify them by cooking the clams over our open wood-burning fire in the Tavern. It took a number of tries to get it right. I chop the clams first and then add scallops for their sweetness and irresistible flavor. In fact, the dish has become so popular that, along with Roasted Oysters, it's often the first thing that our staff and regulars order when they come to the Tavern. Baked clams are great for parties: you can assemble them up to a day ahead, refrigerate, and then cook them when you're ready—in a baking pan in the oven or directly on the grates of a hot grill.

In a large pot, bring the wine, 1 cup water, the sliced shallot, 2 of the smashed garlic cloves, and the parsley stems to a boil over high heat. Add the clams, cover the pot, and steam until they open, 6 to 8 minutes. Using a slotted spoon, transfer the clams to a large bowl and discard the sediment.

Remove the clams from the shells and save half the shells. Cut the clams into quarters and transfer to a small bowl; cover and refrigerate. Separate the 10 reserved shells and rinse them. Strain the broth into a small container.

Make the filling. In a large skillet, heat 2 tablespoons of the oil and 2 tablespoons of the butter over medium-low heat. Add the onions, leeks, minced shallots, minced garlic, ginger, and 1 teaspoon of the thyme and cook until the onions are softened, 12 minutes. Reduce the heat, pour in the reserved clam broth, and simmer until the pan is almost dry. Season with salt and pepper. Transfer the onion mixture to a large bowl and set aside to cool.

In a large skillet, heat the remaining 2 tablespoons oil and remaining 2 tablespoons butter over medium heat. Add the panko, the remaining teaspoon of thyme, and the remaining smashed garlic clove and toast, stirring constantly, until golden brown, about 4 minutes. Season with salt, discard the garlic, and transfer the panko to a medium bowl.

To finish the filling, add the clams, scallops, chopped parsley, and lemon juice to the onion mixture, season with salt and pepper, and mix well.

Preheat the oven to 375°F. To keep the clams from tipping, spread the rock salt in a large baking pan.

Gently pack the filling into the reserved shells. Cover the packed clam shells evenly with the browned panko, lightly patting to help them stick. Nestle the clams in the salt. Bake just until hot, 15 to 20 minutes. Serve with the lemon wedges.

FLOUNDER WITH MARINATED CUCUMBERS & YOGURT SAUCE

Serves **4**

- **3** small cucumbers
- **2** tablespoons plus 1 teaspoon white balsamic vinegar
- **2** tablespoons plus 1 teaspoon fresh lime juice
- **2** tablespoons fresh lemon juice
- **1** teaspoon finely chopped dill

Salt and pepper

- **½** cup Greek yogurt
- **¼** teaspoon honey
- **2** teaspoons finely chopped cilantro
- **1** teaspoon finely chopped mint
- **1** teaspoon finely chopped tarragon

Four 6-ounce skinless flounder fillets

- **1** tablespoon olive oil

Extra-virgin olive oil

- **1** tablespoon finely chopped chives

Editor's Wine Choice
Zesty, refreshing Grüner Veltliner:
2013 Etz Grüner

All of the elements of this dish—the crunchy cucumber salad and creamy yogurt sauce—are meant to be chilled except for the flounder served straight from the pan. I prefer to make the salad with Persian cucumbers because I like their small size and lack of seeds; and their skins aren't bitter, so you don't have to peel them. If you can find Mexican gherkins (they look like tiny watermelons, at right), they make a nice addition.

Using a mandoline or a sharp knife, cut 2 of the cucumbers lengthwise into very thin, supple slices; discard the first and last slices, which will be mostly skin. In a large bowl, combine the sliced cucumbers with 2 tablespoons of the vinegar, 2 tablespoons of the lime juice, the lemon juice, and dill and season with salt and pepper. Toss gently to coat the cucumbers; marinate for about 30 minutes.

Meanwhile, peel the remaining cucumber, halve lengthwise, seed, and slice. Set aside.

In a small bowl, combine the yogurt, 2 tablespoons water, the remaining 1 teaspoon vinegar and 1 teaspoon lime juice, the honey, 1 teaspoon of the cilantro, the mint, and tarragon. Stir until you have a smooth, spreadable sauce, thinning it with a bit more water if necessary. Season with salt and pepper, cover, and refrigerate.

Season the flounder with salt and pepper. In a large nonstick skillet, heat the olive oil over medium heat. Lay the fillets in the pan and cook until lightly browned on the bottom, about 3 minutes. Flip the fillets and cook until just cooked through, about a minute more.

While the fish is cooking, season the sliced cucumber with extra-virgin olive oil, salt, and pepper.

Spread a large spoonful of the yogurt sauce in the middle of each plate. Drain the marinated cucumbers, pat dry, and mound on the sauce. Top with the flounder fillets, spoon the sliced cucumbers over the fish, and scatter the chives and the remaining 1 teaspoon cilantro on top.

CHOCOLATE BREAD PUDDING

Makes **one 9-by-13-inch pan**

Unsalted butter for the pan

3 cups heavy cream

2 cups whole milk

1½ cups sugar

1 vanilla bean, split lengthwise

4 large eggs

2 large egg yolks

4 ounces bittersweet chocolate, melted in a small bowl

¾ teaspoon vanilla extract

1 pound brioche, crusts removed and cut into ¾-inch cubes

2 ounces bittersweet chocolate pieces (about ⅓ cup)

2 ounces milk chocolate pieces (about ⅓ cup)

1 cup heavy cream, lightly whipped (optional)

Bread pudding is a way for an inexperienced cook to feel triumphant and an experienced cook to feel deeply satisfied by making something wonderful from leftovers. Brioche works best, but you can use challah or croissants. Bread pudding reheats really well, and it's even good cold for breakfast. I like it with homemade ice cream or whipped cream.

Preheat the oven to 325°F, with a rack in the middle position. Butter a 9-by-13-inch baking pan.

In a large pot, combine the cream, 1 cup of the milk, and the sugar. Scrape the seeds from the vanilla bean into the pot, then toss in the bean. Bring the mixture to a boil over medium heat, whisking until the sugar dissolves. Discard the vanilla bean.

Meanwhile, in a medium bowl, combine the remaining 1 cup milk, the eggs, and yolks and whisk until smooth.

When the cream mixture boils, remove it from the heat and steadily whisk about a cup of the liquid into the egg mixture to temper it. Pour the egg mixture back into the pot, whisking constantly. Gradually whisk about a cup of the egg mixture into the bowl of melted chocolate, then pour the chocolate mixture back into the pot, whisking constantly. Whisk in the vanilla extract. Add the brioche to the pot and stir the chocolate mixture well to break up the bread. Let the mixture stand for about 30 minutes so the brioche can absorb the liquid.

Pour the brioche mixture into the buttered pan. Sprinkle the bittersweet and milk chocolate pieces on top. Bake the bread pudding until it's just set, 45 to 55 minutes; when it is ready, the pudding will puff up. Let the pudding cool for about 15 minutes before serving. Serve with the whipped cream, if you like.

Brioche helps make this dessert buttery, sweet and rich.

SCALLOPS WITH ORANGE SAUCE

Total **45 min**
Serves **4 as a first course**

ORANGE SAUCE

- 1 **tablespoon unsalted butter**
- 2 **tablespoons extra-virgin olive oil**
- 1 **large sea scallop, cut into ½-inch pieces**
- 2 **tablespoons Pernod**
- 1 **cup fresh orange juice**
- 1 **teaspoon finely chopped peeled fresh ginger**
- 1 **small tarragon sprig**

One 2-inch piece of orange peel

1½ teaspoons fresh lemon juice

Kosher salt

- 2 **oranges**

SCALLOPS

12 **large sea scallops**

Kosher salt and pepper

- 2 **tablespoons extra-virgin olive oil**
- 2 **tablespoons unsalted butter, cubed**
- 2 **garlic cloves**
- 2 **thyme sprigs**

Chopped tarragon, for garnish

Editor's Wine Choice
Full-bodied, Rhône-style white:
2011 Andrew Rich Roussanne

Anthony conceived of this recipe when his local Peconic Bay scallops were in season just as citrus was hitting its peak on the East Coast. For the orange sauce, he adds a double hit of anise flavor with Pernod and fresh tarragon.

1. Make the orange sauce In a medium saucepan, melt the butter in 1 tablespoon of the olive oil. Add the scallop pieces and cook over moderate heat, stirring, until the scallop and butter are golden, about 4 minutes. Add the Pernod and cook, scraping up any browned bits from the bottom of the pan, until reduced to a glaze, about 3 minutes. Add the orange juice and ginger and bring to a boil. Simmer over moderately high heat, stirring occasionally, until reduced to ⅔ cup, about 5 minutes. Remove from the heat and add the tarragon sprig and orange peel. Let stand for 5 minutes, then discard the tarragon and orange peel. Transfer the sauce to a blender and puree until smooth. Strain the sauce through a fine sieve into a medium bowl. Stir in the lemon juice and remaining 1 tablespoon of olive oil and season with salt.

2. Using a very sharp knife, peel the oranges, being sure to remove all of the bitter white pith. Working over a small bowl to catch the juices, cut in between the membranes to release the sections.

3. Prepare the scallops Season the scallops with salt and pepper. In a large skillet, heat the olive oil until shimmering. Add the scallops and cook over high heat until browned on the bottom, about 2 minutes. Flip the scallops and add the butter, garlic and thyme. Cook over high heat, basting the scallops with the melted butter, until nearly cooked through, about 2 minutes longer.

4. Divide the orange sauce among 4 plates and top with the scallops and orange segments. Garnish with chopped tarragon and serve right away.

For more on Michael Anthony
gramercytavern.com
Gramercy Tavern
@chefmikeanthony

COFFEE WALNUT
LOAF, P.24

ANNIE BELL'S BAKING BIBLE

Over 200 Triple-Tested Recipes That You'll Want to Cook Again and Again

BY **ANNIE BELL**

BRITISH food writer Annie Bell is frustrated with what she sees as the ongoing trend in cake-making–"more icing, more frills, ever prettier," she says–so she's written a comprehensive book of "unapologetically classic" recipes. Some are basic, some are "less fashionable," but all are the desserts she goes back to again and again. She offers one fail-safe recipe after another, from classics like Proust's madeleines and jam-filled Bakewell slices (page 28) to some more novel creations, like her soft-bake chocolate and fennel cookies (page 25). Bell's goal is for the book to be useful above all else, and in that spirit she avoids specialized pastry equipment and hard-to-find ingredients. She assures that if you want to bake, you can.

Published by Kyle Books, $35

COFFEE WALNUT LOAF

Makes **one 9-inch loaf**

EQUIPMENT

9-inch/5½-cup nonstick loaf pan, electric mixer, wire rack, offset spatula

FOR THE CAKE

1¾ cups self-rising flour

1 cup light brown sugar

½ teaspoon sea salt

1 cup canola oil

4 large eggs, separated

¼ cup strong black coffee, cold

¼ cup whole milk

⅔ cup chopped walnuts

FOR THE COFFEE CREAM

½ cup mascarpone

2 teaspoons strong black coffee, cold

1 teaspoon light corn syrup

1 teaspoon confectioners' sugar, sifted

FOR THE ICING

100 grams (¾ cup plus 1 tablespoon) confectioners' sugar, sifted

1 to 2 tablespoons strong black coffee, cold

LITTLE EXTRAS

Unsalted butter for greasing

6 to 8 walnut halves for decorating

Confectioners' sugar for dusting

Sister of date and walnut, coffee is the other flavor that harmonizes with this aromatic but slightly bitter nut. You could also fill this with a buttercream rather than the mascarpone suggested, or simply ice the top if you are after something plainer.

Preheat the oven to 325°F convection oven/375°F conventional oven, and butter a 9-inch/5½-cup nonstick loaf pan. Sift the flour, sugar, and salt into a large bowl. Add the oil, the egg yolks, coffee, and milk and beat with a wooden spoon until smooth. Whisk the egg whites until stiff in a large bowl using an electric mixer and fold into the mixture in two batches.

Stir in the walnuts and transfer the mixture to the loaf pan, smoothing the surface. Give the pan several sharp taps on the work surface to bring up any large air bubbles. Bake for 50 to 55 minutes until a skewer inserted into the center comes out clean. Leave the cake to cool in the pan for a few minutes, and then run a knife around the edge and turn out onto a wire rack. Place it the right way up and leave to cool. If not icing it right away, wrap it in plastic wrap.

To make the coffee cream, spoon the mascarpone into a bowl and beat in the coffee, then the corn syrup and confectioners' sugar. Slit the cake in half, about two-thirds of the way up the sides to account for the risen dome. Spread the cream over the lower half and sandwich with the top.

To make the icing, blend the confectioners' sugar and coffee together in a bowl and drizzle down the center of the cake, smoothing it toward the sides using an offset spatula. Don't worry about completely covering the surface or about it trickling down the sides. Decorate the surface with the walnut halves and then dust with a little confectioners' sugar. Leave to set for 1 hour.

SOFT-BAKE CHOCOLATE & FENNEL COOKIES

Makes **approximately 20 cookies**

EQUIPMENT

2 nonstick baking sheets, food processor, mortar and pestle, offset spatula

FOR THE COOKIES

9 tablespoons unsalted butter, diced

1 cup superfine sugar

1 large egg

½ teaspoon vanilla extract

1 cup almond flour

⅔ cup all-purpose flour, sifted

1 teaspoon baking powder, sifted

1 heaping teaspoon fennel seeds

¾ cup dried apricots, chopped

7 ounces dark chocolate (approximately 70 percent cocoa solids), coarsely chopped

LITTLE EXTRAS

Unsalted butter for greasing

I love dreaming up slightly outlandish combinations of flavors, and cookies in particular allow for this. There is something in their character that accommodates a bold hand–dark chocolate, apricot and fennel? It works, I promise you. These blowsy, amorphous cookies are crisp around the edges and chewy within. They look something like a treasure island map with their nooks and crannies.

Preheat the oven to 400°F convection oven/425°F conventional oven and butter a couple of nonstick baking sheets. Cream the butter and sugar together in a food processor, then beat in the egg and vanilla extract. Add the almond flour, all-purpose flour, and baking powder and process to a soft dough. Transfer the mixture to a large bowl.

Coarsely grind the fennel seeds in a mortar and pestle, and stir into the cookie batter with the apricots and chocolate.

Drop generous heaping teaspoons of the mixture onto the baking sheets, spacing them well apart—I allow about six per sheet—and cook them in two batches. Bake for 8 to 10 minutes until golden around the edges but pale within. The lower baking sheet may take a little longer than the top. Leave the cookies to cool for 3 minutes, then loosen them with an offset spatula and leave to cool completely. They are at their best the day they are made, while the chocolate is gooey and the outside crisp.

NEW YORK CHEESECAKE

Makes **one 9-inch cheesecake**

EQUIPMENT

9-inch nonstick cake pan with a removable base, 3 inches deep; food processor; foil

FOR THE PASTRY

⅔ **cup all-purpose flour, sifted**

½ **cup almond flour**

¼ **cup superfine sugar**

6 **tablespoons unsalted butter, melted**

FOR THE FILLING

3⅔ **cups cream cheese**

1⅓ **cups superfine sugar**

2 **large eggs, and 1 egg yolk**

1¾ **cups heavy cream**

⅓ **cup all-purpose flour, sifted**

1½ **teaspoons vanilla extract**

Freshly grated nutmeg

LITTLE EXTRAS

Mixture of fresh berries, e.g. halved or small strawberries, raspberries, blueberries (optional)

Confectioners' sugar for dusting (optional)

Author's Tip Cheesecakes are one of the best keepers among cakes. A cheesecake needs to mature before you can eat it; there is no digging in right away. Be sure to cover it with foil when chilling overnight to allow it to breathe; plastic wrap will create a wet environment. Probably the best time to make it is during the afternoon so it will be ready for mid-morning coffee the next day. As an alternative to fresh fruit you could include 1 cup raisins with the filling.

Many years ago, my husband's love of cheesecake rallied me into trying to produce something as delectable as the one he recalled from his childhood. I lost count of how many we went through before hitting on a formula that lived up to the hallowed memory—somehow either the crust was out of kilter, the filling not quite as he remembered it, or the distribution of raisins just not right. But eventually we settled on this as "the one."

The filling is one for hot debate, and it depends on how you like it. My preference is for a really creamy, loosely set filling rather than a drier one, and there is little to this other than cream cheese cut with heavy cream and just a couple of eggs to hold it all together. But the final touch, and one that transports me back to the village bakery of my own childhood—to warm cakes and custard tarts—is a liberal grating of fresh nutmeg.

Preheat the oven to 300°F convection oven/325°F conventional oven. Mix the ingredients for the pastry together in a bowl. Using your fingers, press the mixture onto the bottom of a 9-inch nonstick cake pan with a removable base, 3 inches deep. Bake for 20 to 25 minutes until pale gold, then set aside to cool.

Preheat the oven to 350°F convection oven/400°F conventional oven. To make the filling, blend the cream cheese and sugar in a food processor. Add the eggs, extra yolk, and cream and process briefly. Fold in the flour with the vanilla extract. Carefully pour the mixture into the pan and liberally dust the surface with freshly grated nutmeg. Bake in the oven for 1 hour until puffy around the edges and just set. It should wobble slightly if you move it from side to side. Leave the cheesecake to cool, and then run a knife around the sides and loosely cover the whole thing with foil (but not plastic wrap). Chill overnight.

If wished, to serve, pile a mixture of berries in the center of the cheesecake and dust with confectioners' sugar. Accompany with extra berries.

Almond
flour makes
the crust
more
flavorful.

BAKEWELL SLICES

Makes **12 slices**

EQUIPMENT

Food processor; plastic wrap; 9-inch nonstick square brownie pan, 2 inches deep; parchment paper; baking beans or dried beans

FOR THE PASTRY

- 4 tablespoons unsalted butter, diced
- ½ cup confectioners' sugar
- 1 large egg yolk
- 1 cup all-purpose flour

FOR THE FILLING

- 5½ tablespoons unsalted butter, diced
- 1 cup superfine sugar
- 3 large eggs
- ½ teaspoon almond extract
- 2 cups almond flour
- 1 teaspoon baking powder, sifted
- ½ cup raspberry or cherry jam
- ⅓ cup sliced almonds

LITTLE EXTRAS

All-purpose flour for rolling

Confectioners' sugar for dusting

A thick bank of delicate almond cake with a jam tart below, a much-loved British classic. The real thing is subtly flavored with almond extract; there should be just enough to spar with the jam.

To make the pastry, cream the butter and confectioners' sugar together in a food processor. Mix in the egg yolk, then add the flour. As soon as the dough comes together in a ball, wrap it in plastic wrap and chill for at least 2 hours; it can be kept in the fridge for several days.

Preheat the oven to 325°F convection oven/375°F conventional oven. Thinly roll out the pastry on a lightly floured surface and use it to line the base of a 9-inch nonstick square brownie pan, 2 inches deep, draping the excess up the sides; don't worry if you end up having to patch it as this won't show.

Line the pastry case with parchment paper and weight it with baking beans or dried beans. Cook for 15 to 20 minutes until lightly colored, then remove the paper and beans, and trim the sides to leave you with a tightly fitting base.

To make the filling, cream the butter and sugar together in a food processor, then add the eggs one at a time, then the almond extract, almond flour, and baking powder.

Spread the pastry base with the jam, then spoon the almond mixture on top. Carefully smooth the surface, taking care not to blend it with the jam, and scatter in the almonds. Bake in the oven for 25 to 30 minutes until golden and risen. Run a knife around the edge and leave to cool in the pan.

To serve, dust with confectioners' sugar, cut in half, and slice into 12 bars, or half this size if wished. It will be quite crumbly when very fresh and should keep well for several days in an airtight container.

Both the filling
and pastry
are easy to
make in a food
processor.

ORANGE & FENNEL GRAVLAX

Active **20 min**; Total **3 days**
Serves **10 to 12**

GRAVLAX

⅓ cup kosher salt

¼ cup sugar

1½ tablespoons finely grated
   orange zest

1 tablespoon fennel seeds, crushed

One 2-pound tail-end salmon fillet
   with skin, halved lengthwise and
   pin bones removed

3 tablespoons chopped dill

Lemon wedges and rye bread slices
   or Little Gem lettuce leaves, for
   serving

MUSTARD SAUCE

½ cup sour cream

2 tablespoons Dijon mustard

2 tablespoons stone-ground
   mustard

Kosher salt and pepper

"Of all the cured delicacies to make at home, this is far and away the simplest," Bell says. "It requires no special equipment or complicated technique, just time and a few everyday ingredients." Another bonus according to Bell: The gravlax freezes beautifully, sliced or unsliced.

1. Make the gravlax On a work surface, lay out a piece of plastic wrap several inches longer than the salmon fillet. In a small bowl, combine the salt, sugar, orange zest and fennel seeds and mix well. Sprinkle one-quarter of the spice mix down the middle of the plastic wrap, then lay 1 piece of the salmon on top of it, skin side down. Scatter two-thirds of the remaining spice mix on the salmon, concentrating it where the fish is thickest. Lay the second piece of salmon on top, skin side up, so that the flesh sides are touching. Sprinkle the remaining spice mix on top, wrap the fish tightly in the plastic, then wrap in a second layer of plastic.

2. Place the fish in a large cast-iron skillet and set a smaller cast-iron skillet on top to weight it down. Refrigerate for 3 days, flipping the fish every 12 hours, until it feels somewhat firm and looks cured in the center.

3. Make the mustard sauce In a medium bowl, combine the sour cream and both mustards. Season with salt and pepper and mix well. Refrigerate until ready to serve.

4. Rinse the spice mix off the fish and pat dry with paper towels. Transfer the gravlax to a platter and sprinkle with the dill, gently pressing to help it adhere. Thinly slice the gravlax and serve with the mustard sauce, lemon wedges and bread slices or lettuce leaves.

MAKE AHEAD The gravlax can be tightly wrapped and refrigerated for up to 1 week or frozen for up to 2 weeks. The mustard sauce can be refrigerated for up to 3 days.

CARAMEL CASHEW TART, P.34

CARAMEL

BY **CAROLE BLOOM**

WHEN anyone asks Carole Bloom for the best dinner-party dessert, she points them toward caramel–every time. "Caramel is what most of us associate with that wowwee feeling of 'that tastes so amazing!'" she says. In her 11th book on sweets, the pastry chef and oft-praised genius in the dessert world sets out to prove that caramel is just as versatile (and maybe even more tantalizing) than chocolate–and that a little bit makes any dessert better: Bloom's cashew tart (pictured at left), with its chewy center layer of caramel, is like a candy bar in a 9½-inch tart pan. And her cocoa cookies (page 42) are delicious on their own, but with a gooey caramel filling, they are her husband's favorites.

Published by Gibbs Smith, $25

CARAMEL CASHEW TART

Makes **one 9½-inch round tart, 12 to 14 servings**

SPECIAL EQUIPMENT

One 9½-inch round, fluted-edge removable-bottom tart pan

PASTRY DOUGH

1¼ cups (5½ ounces) all-purpose flour

½ cup (1¾ ounces) confectioners' sugar

⅛ teaspoon kosher or fine-grained sea salt

8 tablespoons (4 ounces, 1 stick) unsalted butter, chilled

1 large egg yolk, room temperature

½ teaspoon pure vanilla extract

BITTERSWEET CHOCOLATE GANACHE

6 ounces bittersweet chocolate (66 to 72 percent cacao content), finely chopped

⅔ cup heavy whipping cream

CARAMEL CASHEW FILLING

¾ cup (5 ounces) granulated sugar

¼ cup water

1 tablespoon light corn syrup

⅓ cup heavy whipping cream

6 tablespoons (3 ounces, ¾ stick) unsalted butter, softened

½ teaspoon pure vanilla extract

Pinch of kosher or fine-grained sea salt

1½ cups (6¾ ounces) toasted cashews, coarsely chopped

GARNISH

20 cashew pieces

This tart resembles a candy bar. Two layers of bittersweet chocolate ganache enclose a chewy mixture of caramel and toasted chopped cashews. This all rests on a delicate sweet pastry shell. There are a few steps involved in preparing this tart that can easily be spread out over a couple of days.

Pastry dough Briefly pulse together the flour, sugar, and salt in the work bowl of a food processor fitted with the steel blade. Cut the butter into small pieces and add. Pulse until the butter is cut into very tiny pieces, about 30 seconds. The texture will be sandy with very tiny lumps. In a small bowl, use a fork to beat the egg yolk and vanilla together. With the food processor running, pour this mixture through the feed tube. Process until the dough wraps itself around the blade, about 1 minute. Shape the dough into a flat disk and wrap tightly in a double layer of plastic wrap. Chill in the refrigerator until firm before using, about 2 hours.

Position a rack in the center of the oven and preheat to 375°F. On a smooth, flat surface, roll out the dough between sheets of lightly floured waxed or parchment paper to a large rectangle ¼ inch thick. Peel off the top piece of paper, brush off any excess flour, and gently roll the pastry dough around the rolling pin. Place the tart pan directly under the rolling pin and carefully unroll the dough into the pan. Gently lift up the edges and fit the dough against the bottom and sides of the tart pan, pushing it lightly into the fluted edges. Trim off any excess dough at the top edge of the pan and patch any places that have holes or tears. Place the pan on a baking sheet and freeze for 15 minutes.

Line the shell with a large piece of aluminum foil that fits well against the bottom and sides and fill with tart weights. Bake the shell for 10 minutes, then remove the foil and weights. Lightly pierce the bottom of the shell with a fork to release air and prevent it from puffing up. Bake another 12 to 15 minutes, until light golden and set. Remove the baking sheet from the oven and transfer the tart pan to a rack to cool completely.

Bittersweet chocolate ganache Place the chocolate in a large bowl. Heat the cream in a small saucepan until bubbles form around the edges. Pour the cream over the chocolate and let stand for 30 seconds. Stir the cream and chocolate together with a heat-resistant spatula until completely melted and smooth. Pour half of this mixture into the cooled tart shell. Cover the bowl with the remaining ganache tightly with plastic wrap and hold at room temperature. Place the tart shell in the refrigerator to set the filling, 30 to 45 minutes.

Caramel cashew filling Combine the sugar, water, and corn syrup in a 3-quart heavy-duty saucepan. Stir over medium-high heat to dissolve the sugar. Brush the sides of the pan with a pastry brush dipped in water and cook the mixture, without stirring, until it turns amber colored, about 8 minutes. At the same time heat the cream to a boil in a small saucepan.

When the caramel mixture turns amber, add the hot cream, butter, vanilla, and salt and stir constantly. Be careful because the mixture will bubble and foam. When the butter is completely melted, add the toasted cashews and stir to coat them completely with the caramel mixture. Pour the mixture into a large bowl and chill in the refrigerator until cool and spreadable, about 15 minutes.

Pour the caramel cashew filling over the chocolate ganache in the tart shell, spreading it evenly.

Warm the remaining chocolate ganache in a small saucepan over low heat or in a microwave-safe bowl on low power for 30 second bursts, stirring often, until the mixture is fluid. Pour the ganache over the caramel cashew filling and spread it out evenly.

GARNISH Place the cashew pieces close together around the outer edges of the tart, or coarsely chop and sprinkle over the top. Chill the tart for 45 minutes to 1 hour, until firm, but not hard. Serve slices of the tart at room temperature.

KEEPING Store the tart on a plate lightly covered with waxed paper, then tightly wrapped in aluminum foil, in the refrigerator for up to 3 days.

STREAMLINING The pastry dough can be made up to 4 days in advance and kept tightly wrapped in plastic wrap in the refrigerator. To freeze for up to 3 months, place it in a freezer-safe bag. Label and date the package. If frozen, defrost overnight in the refrigerator and bring to room temperature before using. The pastry dough can be baked up to 2 days in advance and kept tightly wrapped in aluminum foil at room temperature.

MAKING A CHANGE Replace the cashews with walnuts or pecans.

ESPRESSO CRÈME CARAMEL

Makes **6 servings**

SPECIAL EQUIPMENT

Six ½-cup ramekins, custard cups, or bowls and one 3-quart baking dish

ESPRESSO CRÈME CARAMEL

⅔ **cup (4 ounces) granulated sugar**

⅓ **cup water**

1½ **cups milk (whole or 2 percent)**

½ **cup heavy whipping cream**

¼ **teaspoon kosher or fine-grained sea salt**

2 **teaspoons instant espresso powder**

2 **large eggs, room temperature**

2 **large egg yolks, room temperature**

½ **teaspoon pure vanilla extract**

½ **cup (3½ ounces) granulated sugar**

1 **quart boiling water**

For coffee lovers this is the ultimate, intense caramel flavor with a shot of espresso. To assure the silkiness of the custard, make certain to stir constantly when mixing the hot milk into the egg mixture. The color of the custard and flow of the caramel make this dessert eye pleasing and mouthwatering.

Position a rack in the center of the oven and preheat to 350°F. Place the ramekins in the baking dish.

Combine the sugar and water in a small saucepan over medium-high heat. Bring the mixture to a boil. Cook, without stirring, until the mixture turns a rich golden brown, about 8 minutes. Divide the caramel evenly between the ramekins. Tilt and rotate each ramekin so the caramel completely covers the bottoms.

Warm the milk, cream, and salt in a 2-quart heavy-duty saucepan over medium heat until tiny bubbles form around the edges. Add the espresso powder and stir until it is completely dissolved, about 1 minute. Remove from the heat and cover the mixture to keep it warm for a few minutes.

Whip the eggs, egg yolks, and vanilla in the bowl of an electric stand mixer using the wire whip attachment, or in a large bowl using a hand-held mixer, until frothy. Slowly sprinkle on the sugar and whisk until well blended. In a steady stream, pour in the hot milk and mix thoroughly.

Strain the custard into a bowl or large liquid measuring cup. Pour the custard into the caramel-lined ramekins, dividing it evenly among them, and filling them almost to the top.

Place the baking dish on the oven rack. Carefully pour the water into the baking dish until it reaches halfway up the sides of the ramekins.

Bake for 30 minutes, until a toothpick or cake tester inserted in the center comes out clean. Remove the baking dish from the oven. Using a pair of tongs, remove the ramekins from the water bath and place them on a rack to cool completely. Cover the ramekins tightly with plastic wrap and chill in the refrigerator for several hours or overnight.

To unmold the custards, gently run a thin-blade knife around the sides of the ramekins. Place a serving plate over the top and invert the custard onto the plate. Repeat with each custard. Serve the custards cool.

KEEPING Store the baked custard in the ramekins, tightly covered with a double layer of plastic wrap, in the refrigerator for up to 3 days.

MAKING A CHANGE To intensify the espresso flavor, increase the instant espresso powder to 1 tablespoon.

CHOCOLATE CUPCAKES WITH SALTED CARAMEL BUTTERCREAM FROSTING

Makes **24 cupcakes**

SPECIAL EQUIPMENT

Candy thermometer and two 12-cavity muffin pans

CUPCAKES

- 6 ounces unsweetened chocolate, finely chopped
- 1¾ cups (7¾ ounces) cake flour
- 1 teaspoon baking soda
- ½ teaspoon kosher or fine-grained sea salt
- 8 tablespoons (4 ounces, 1 stick) unsalted butter, softened
- 1 cup (6½ ounces) superfine sugar
- ⅔ cup (4 ounces) firmly packed light brown sugar
- 2 large eggs, room temperature
- 1 teaspoon pure vanilla extract
- 2 teaspoons pure chocolate extract
- 1 cup sour cream

These scrumptious cupcakes are made with unsweetened chocolate and are frosted with caramel buttercream that is made with Fleur de Sel sea salt. The caramel sauce used to flavor the buttercream can be made as long as a week in advance.

Position the racks to the upper and lower thirds of the oven and preheat to 350°F. Line the pans with cupcake papers.

Cupcakes Melt the chocolate in the top of a double boiler over low heat, stirring often with a rubber spatula to help melt evenly. Or melt the chocolate in a microwave oven on low power for 30 second bursts. Stir with a rubber spatula after each burst to help melt evenly.

In a small bowl, sift the cake flour and baking soda together. Add the salt and toss to blend.

Beat the butter in the bowl of an electric stand mixer using the flat beater attachment, or in a large bowl using a hand-held mixer on medium speed, until light and fluffy, about 2 minutes. Add the sugars and beat together well on medium speed. Stop occasionally and scrape down the sides and bottom of the mixing bowl with a rubber spatula.

Using a fork, lightly beat the eggs with the vanilla and chocolate extracts in a small bowl. Add to the butter mixture and mix together, stopping a few times to scrape down the sides and bottom of the mixing bowl. At first the mixture may look curdled as the eggs are added, but as you stop and scrape down the bowl, the mixture will smooth out.

Alternately add the flour mixture and the sour cream, in 4 or 5 stages, mixing well after each addition. Stop after each addition and scrape down the bottom and sides of the bowl with a rubber spatula. Add the melted chocolate to the mixture and blend together thoroughly.

Use a 2-inch ice cream scoop to divide the batter evenly among the cavities in the pans. Bake the cupcakes for 8 minutes, switch the pans on the oven racks, and bake another 8 minutes, until a cake tester inserted in the center comes out clean. Remove the pans from the oven and cool completely on racks.

SALTED CARAMEL SAUCE

- ¾ **cup heavy whipping cream**
- 1 **cup (6½ ounces) granulated sugar**
- ¼ **cup water**
- 1 **tablespoon light corn syrup**
- 4 **tablespoons (2 ounces, ½ stick) unsalted butter, softened**
- 1½ **teaspoons pure vanilla extract**
- 1 **teaspoon Fleur de Sel salt**

BUTTERCREAM FROSTING

- 2 **large eggs, room temperature**
- 2 **large egg yolks, room temperature**
- 1½ **cups (10 ounces) granulated sugar, divided**
- ½ **cup water**
- ¼ **teaspoon cream of tartar**
- 16 **tablespoons (8 ounces, 2 sticks) unsalted butter, softened**

GARNISH

- 2 **teaspoons Fleur de Sel or other fine finishing salt**

Salted caramel sauce Place the cream in a small saucepan and warm over medium heat until bubbles form at the edges.

While the cream is heating, combine the sugar, water, and corn syrup in a 2-quart heavy-duty saucepan. Cook over high heat, without stirring, until the mixture begins to boil. Brush around the inside of the pan with a damp pastry brush at the point where the sugar syrup meets the sides of the pan. Do this twice during the cooking process to prevent the sugar from crystallizing. Cook the mixture over high heat, without stirring, until it turns amber colored, about 10 minutes.

Stir in the hot cream using a long-handle heat-resistant spatula. Be very careful because it will bubble and foam. Stir to dissolve any lumps. Add the butter to the caramel mixture and stir until it is melted. Remove the saucepan from the heat and stir in the vanilla and salt. Transfer the caramel sauce to a container and cover tightly. Let the sauce cool, then chill in the refrigerator until it is thick, about 2 hours.

Buttercream frosting Whip the eggs, egg yolks, and ¼ cup of the sugar in the bowl of an electric stand mixer using the wire whip attachment, or in a large bowl using a hand-held mixer, until they are very pale colored and hold a slowly dissolving ribbon as the beater is lifted, about 5 minutes.

While the eggs are whipping, place the remaining sugar, water, and cream of tartar in a 2-quart heavy-duty saucepan. Bring the mixture to a boil, without stirring. Brush around the inside of the pan with a damp pastry brush at the point where the sugar syrup meets the sides of the pan. Do this twice during the cooking process to prevent the sugar from crystallizing. Cook over high heat, without stirring, until the mixture registers 242°F on a candy thermometer (soft ball stage). Immediately remove the thermometer and place it in a glass of warm water, then remove the pan from the heat so it won't continue to cook.

Adjust the mixer speed to low and pour the sugar syrup into the whipped eggs in a slow, steady stream. Aim the sugar syrup between the beater and the side of the bowl, so it doesn't get caught up in the beater or thrown against the sides of the bowl. Turn the mixer speed up to medium high and whip until the bowl is cool to the touch, about 8 minutes.

continued on page 40

CHOCOLATE CUPCAKES WITH SALTED CARAMEL BUTTERCREAM FROSTING *continued*

Adjust the mixer speed to medium and add the butter, 2 tablespoons at a time. Continue to beat until the mixture is thoroughly blended and fluffy. Add the cooled caramel sauce and stir until it is thoroughly blended.

Use a small spatula to frost the top of each cupcake with about 2 tablespoons of the frosting. You can also pipe the frosting onto the cupcakes in a decorative design. Sprinkle the top of each cupcake with a few grains of Fleur de Sel or other fine finishing salt. Serve the cupcakes at room temperature.

KEEPING Store the unfrosted cupcakes tightly wrapped in aluminum foil for up to 3 days at room temperature. Store the frosted cupcakes in a single layer in an airtight plastic container in the refrigerator for up to 4 days. To freeze for up to 4 months, wrap the cakes tightly in several layers of plastic wrap and aluminum foil. Label and date the package. If frozen, defrost overnight in the refrigerator and bring to room temperature before serving.

MAKING A CHANGE Add ⅔ cup toasted and coarsely chopped walnuts or pecans to the cupcake batter after adding the chocolate.

STREAMLINING The caramel sauce can be prepared up to a week in advance and kept in a tightly covered container in the refrigerator. If it is too firm, soften it on low power in a microwave oven for 20 second bursts.

The Buttercream Frosting can be prepared up to 3 days in advance and kept in an airtight plastic container in the refrigerator or up to 4 months in the freezer. If frozen, defrost overnight in the refrigerator. To re-beat the Buttercream, break it up into chunks and place in a bowl. Place the bowl in a saucepan of warm water and let the Buttercream begin to melt around the bottom. Wipe the bottom of the bowl dry and beat the Buttercream with an electric mixer until it is fluffy and smooth.

COCOA & CARAMEL SANDWICH COOKIES

Makes **about forty 1½-inch sandwich cookies**

SPECIAL EQUIPMENT

Candy thermometer, one 8-inch square baking pan, and 3 baking sheets

COCOA COOKIES

1½ cups (6¾ ounces) all-purpose flour

⅔ cup (2½ ounces) cocoa powder, natural or Dutch processed

¼ teaspoon kosher or fine-grained sea salt

1 cup (6½ ounces) granulated sugar

12 tablespoons (6 ounces, 1½ sticks) unsalted butter, chilled

1 large egg, room temperature

½ teaspoon pure vanilla extract

CARAMEL FILLING

Nonstick baking spray

2¼ cups (14½ ounces) granulated sugar

1¾ cups heavy whipping cream

⅓ cup honey

1 tablespoon light corn syrup

4 tablespoons (2 ounces, ½ stick) unsalted butter, cut into small pieces

Pinch of kosher or fine-grained sea salt

1 tablespoon pure vanilla extract

These tasty sandwich cookies are crunchy and gooey. The cookies, made with cocoa powder, add a bitter yet mildly sweet flavor to the rich-cream honey-based caramel filling. Because the caramel from one cookie may slightly ooze out and stick to another cookie, be careful not to set them too close to each other. These are my husband's favorites with a cold glass of milk.

Cocoa cookies Briefly pulse the flour, cocoa powder, salt, and sugar in the work bowl of a food processor fitted with the steel blade. Cut the butter into small pieces and add. Pulse until the butter is cut into tiny pieces.

Use a fork to lightly beat together the egg and vanilla in a small bowl. With the food processor running, pour this mixture through the feed tube. Process until the dough wraps itself around the blade, about 1 minute. Shape the dough into a flat disk and cover tightly with plastic wrap. Chill until firm, about 3 hours.

Caramel filling Line the baking pan with aluminum foil that fits snugly and hangs a bit over the edges. Spray with nonstick baking spray.

Place the sugar, cream, honey, and corn syrup in a 3-quart heavy-duty saucepan over medium heat. Stir to dissolve the sugar. Increase the heat to medium high, place the candy thermometer in the pan, and cook, without stirring, until the mixture registers 250°F. Turn off the heat and stir in the butter until it is completely melted, then add the salt and vanilla and blend well. Turn the caramel into the prepared pan and place the pan on a wire rack to cool completely.

Position the racks to the upper and lower thirds of the oven and preheat to 400°F. Line the baking sheets with parchment paper or non-stick liners. Roll out the cookie dough between sheets of lightly floured waxed or parchment paper to ¼ inch thick. Use a 1½-inch plain round cutter to cut out the cookies. Place them on the baking sheets, leaving about an inch of space between them. Gather the scraps back together, roll out, and cut out more cookies.

continued on page 44

These crisp cookies are fantastic even without the filling.

COCOA & CARAMEL
SANDWICH COOKIES *continued*

Bake for 6 minutes. Switch the baking sheets on the oven racks and bake another 6 minutes, until set. Remove the baking sheets from the oven and completely cool the cookies on the baking sheets on racks. Lift the cookies from the parchment paper and turn half of them with their bottoms facing up.

Lift the caramel from the pan using the edges of the foil. Use a 1-inch plain round cutter to cut out disks of the caramel. Place a caramel disk on the flat side of one cookie and top it with another cookie, pressing down lightly. If there are not enough caramel disks, gather some of the caramel together and press it into flat disks. Serve the cookies at room temperature.

KEEPING Store the cookies without the filling tightly covered with aluminum foil, at room temperature, for up to 3 days. Store the filled cookies tightly covered with foil, at room temperature, for up to 2 days.

STREAMLINING The cocoa cookie dough can be kept tightly covered in the refrigerator for up to 4 days before baking.

CHOCOLATE CARAMELS

Total **30 min plus 3 hr cooling**
Makes **about 5 dozen caramels**

Vegetable oil, for greasing the pan

1½ cups heavy cream

10 ounces bittersweet chocolate
    (66 to 72 percent cacao
    content), finely chopped

 2 cups sugar

½ cup honey

 2 tablespoons unsalted butter,
    at room temperature

Bloom uses a generous amount of honey in her chocolate caramels, which gives them an aromatic sweetness as well as a soft, sticky consistency. Individually wrapped in parchment paper, the caramels make a lovely gift.

1. Line an 8-inch square baking pan with aluminum foil, extending the foil over the sides of the pan. Using a paper towel, lightly grease the foil with vegetable oil.

2. In a large, heavy-bottomed saucepan, bring the cream to a simmer over moderate heat. Add the chocolate and whisk until melted and smooth. Whisk in the sugar and honey until smooth and bring to a boil; brush down the side of the pan with a damp pastry brush. Continue to cook over moderate heat, stirring frequently, until the temperature reaches 255°F on a candy thermometer, 8 to 10 minutes. Remove the saucepan from the heat and stir in the butter. Pour the caramel into the prepared baking pan and let cool completely, about 3 hours.

3. Invert the caramel onto a parchment-lined cutting board and peel off the foil. Lightly grease the blade of a sharp knife with vegetable oil and cut the caramel into 1-inch squares. Wrap each caramel in a square of parchment paper or a candy wrapper and twist the ends to seal.

MAKE AHEAD The uncut caramel can be tightly wrapped in plastic and refrigerated for up to 2 weeks; cut just before serving. Wrapped caramels can be refrigerated for up to 2 weeks.

For more on Carole Bloom
carolebloom.com

"By exchanging our best cooking tips, we help each other become better weeknight cooks," say Kathy Brennan (left) and Caroline Campion. Here, they fold wontons in Campion's kitchen in Gladstone, New Jersey.

KEEPERS

Two Home Cooks Share
Their Tried & True Weeknight
Recipes & the Secrets to
Happiness in the Kitchen

BY **KATHY BRENNAN** & **CAROLINE CAMPION**

THIS is how food writers Kathy Brennan and Caroline Campion define keeper recipes: "brag-worthy, reliable, crowd-pleasing preparations that we confidently turn to again and again." Their book delivers 120 of them, each with ingenious ways to turn basic ingredients into family-friendly dinners. Their soufflé-like broccoli and cheddar quiche (page 54) is crustless, which is a huge time-saver, and the no-bake skillet lasagna (page 52) is a welcome recipe for anyone cooking for kids. Brennan and Campion also advise how to cure kitchen ennui: by grocery shopping with a friend who cooks completely differently.

Published by Rodale, $27

KALE SALAD WITH POMEGRANATE & PUMPKIN SEEDS

Serves **4**

- 1 **bunch of kale (about ¾ pound), stems and center ribs removed and leaves cut crosswise into 1-inch ribbons**
- 1 **tablespoon olive oil**
- ¼ **teaspoon salt**
- ¼ **cup toasted pumpkin seeds (pepitas)**
- **Seeds from ½ pomegranate (about ½ cup)**
- ½ **tablespoon balsamic vinegar**

Okay, raw kale may not sound all that appetizing, but give this salad a try. Massaging (yes, massaging) the leaves transforms them into soft, silky piles and mellows their sharp, bitter edge. Throw in the pomegranate and pumpkin seeds and you have a very approachable, healthful salad with lots of texture and flavor. If you can find it, use lacinato (also called Tuscan) kale, which is a little sweeter and milder than curly kale, but any variety is fine.

Although seeding pomegranates isn't particularly difficult (see Tip), the convenience of the packaged seeds sold at some stores can't be beat.

In a large bowl, combine the kale, oil, and salt. Using your hands, massage the leaves, rubbing them with the oil and salt until they become softer, smaller, and darker, about 2 minutes. Taste a piece. If it's bitter, massage a little more. Add the pumpkin and pomegranate seeds and gently toss to combine (don't worry if some of the pomegranate seeds burst). Add the vinegar and toss again. Check the seasonings, adding a little more oil and/or vinegar, if needed, and serve.

TIP Our friend Leslie taught us a no-fuss way to remove the seeds from a pomegranate: Cut the fruit in half crosswise. Hold one half in the palm of your nondominant hand over a medium bowl, cut-side down. Firmly whack the skin with the back of a wooden spoon several times. The seeds should start to fall into the bowl. Continue hitting the skin, gently squeezing the pomegranate a little to help the process if needed, until all the seeds are in the bowl. Repeat with the other half, then discard any white pith that may have fallen into the bowl. In addition to being an effective method, it's good therapy if you're in a bad mood—but we'd still advise not wearing your favorite white shirt.

This salad gets better as it sits.

SAUSAGE & WHITE BEAN GRATIN

Serves **6**

⅔ cup panko or regular dried breadcrumbs

2 tablespoons unsalted butter, melted

Salt

2 tablespoons olive oil

1 pound sweet Italian sausages, casings removed

1 small yellow onion, chopped

4 garlic cloves, minced

1 heaping tablespoon tomato paste

1 scant tablespoon fresh thyme leaves or 1 scant teaspoon dried

½ cup dry white wine

1½ cups low-sodium chicken broth

Two 15.5-ounce cans white beans, such as cannellini or Great Northern, drained and rinsed

Pepper

4 large handfuls of baby spinach (optional)

Editor's Wine Choice Medium-bodied, juicy Pinot Noir: 2012 Banshee Sonoma County

There's a lot of wiggle room in this hearty crowd-pleaser. You can cook the sausage and bean mixture a day or two in advance (just allow for extra oven time since it will be cold). If you have an ovenproof pan, such as a cast-iron skillet, you can also use that for the entire recipe. Folding some spinach into the mixture before baking is an easy way to add some color and vegetables, but you can skip it or use other leafy greens, such as Swiss chard, escarole, or broccoli rabe (sturdier ones will need to be blanched first). The gratin also reheats well.

Preheat the oven to 425°F, with a rack in the middle position. In a small bowl, combine the panko and butter, season with salt, and set aside.

In a large skillet, heat the oil over high heat until it shimmers. Add the sausages and cook, stirring often and breaking up the meat, until browned, about 4 minutes. Leaving as much oil in the pan as possible, transfer the sausage to a medium bowl and set aside.

Reduce the heat to medium-low, add the onions and garlic and cook, stirring occasionally, until the onions are softened, about 8 minutes. Add the tomato paste and thyme and stir for about 30 seconds. Add the wine and briskly simmer, scraping up any caramelized bits from the bottom of the pan, until almost evaporated, about 2 minutes.

Add the broth and bring to a simmer, then add the beans, cooked sausage, and any juices. Season with salt and pepper and simmer, stirring occasionally, until heated through and some of the liquid is absorbed, about 5 minutes. The mixture should be wet, but not drowning in liquid. Off the heat, stir in the spinach (if using). Check the seasonings, then transfer the mixture to a 3-quart baking or gratin dish.

Top evenly with the panko mixture and bake until bubbling and the top is golden brown, about 15 minutes. Let rest for 5 to 10 minutes before serving.

SKILLET LASAGNA

Serves **6**

- 2 **tablespoons olive oil**
- 1 **pound sweet or hot Italian sausages, casings removed**
- 1 **small yellow onion, finely chopped**
- 4 **garlic cloves, minced**

Large pinch of hot red pepper flakes

- 1 **teaspoon dried oregano**

Two 28-ounce cans whole, peeled tomatoes

- 1 **sprig basil, plus a handful of basil leaves**

Salt and pepper

One 9-ounce package no-boil lasagna noodles

- 4 **ounces mascarpone cheese or cream cheese (½ cup)**
- ½ **pound fresh mozzarella, thinly sliced and patted dry**

Author's Tip The next time you end up with a crusty or blackened skillet or pot (it happens to everyone), don't sigh and reach for the scouring pad. Just add an inch or so of water and briskly simmer until the stuck-on or burned bits soften and start to come away from the bottom. After the water cools, wash as usual. For real doozies, add a big splash of distilled white vinegar to the water before boiling; after draining the cooled water, scrub with baking soda, then wash. It should be (almost) as good as new.

Editor's Wine Choice Earthy, spicy Sangiovese: 2011 Casamatta Toscana Rosso

Most lasagnas involve a big investment of time and a sink full of pots and pans, but not this one. It has all the pleasures of lasagna—layers of tender noodles, homemade meat sauce, deliciously gooey cheese—but can be whipped up in less than an hour using a single skillet. We're fans of Barilla's no-boil lasagna noodles, but feel free to use whatever brand you like.

In a large high-sided sauté pan with a 3-quart capacity and a lid, heat the oil over high heat until it shimmers. Add the sausages and cook, stirring often and breaking up the meat, until browned, about 4 minutes. Leaving as much oil in the pan as possible, transfer the sausage to a medium bowl and set aside.

Reduce the heat to medium-low, add the onions, garlic, and pepper flakes to the pan, and cook, stirring occasionally, until the onions are softened, about 7 minutes. Add the oregano, the tomatoes and their juices, crushing the tomatoes with your hands or a potato masher, the sprig of basil, and the cooked sausage and any juices. Season with salt and pepper, then gently simmer for 5 minutes, stirring occasionally. Check the seasonings (it should be a little salty) and discard the basil sprig.

Break half of the lasagna noodles in half crosswise (it's fine if smaller pieces break off) and as you do so, push each piece into the sauce under the sausage, distributing them evenly throughout the pan. Break the remaining half of the noodles in half and distribute them evenly over the sauce, then push down on them with the back of a spoon to submerge them. Cover the pan and gently simmer (raising the heat a little, if needed) until the noodles are tender and the sauce has thickened slightly, about 12 minutes.

Dollop the mascarpone over the lasagna and swirl it into the sauce. Top with the mozzarella and gently simmer, covered, until the cheese is melted, about 2 minutes. Off the heat, top with the basil leaves, tearing any large ones. Let the lasagna rest, uncovered, for about 10 minutes, then serve.

This amazing lasagna is made on the stovetop.

CRUSTLESS BROCCOLI & CHEDDAR QUICHE

Makes **one 10-inch quiche**

**Unsalted butter for greasing the
    pie dish**

Salt

3   **cups small broccoli florets (from
    about 1 large head of broccoli)**

1   **cup shredded cheddar cheese
    (about 4 ounces)**

1   **cup whole milk**

⅔ **cup heavy cream**

6   **large eggs**

**Pinch of nutmeg, preferably
    freshly grated**

Pepper

Editor's Wine Choice Ripe,
fruit-forward California
Chardonnay: 2012 Kendall-
Jackson Grand Reserve

The chicest mom Kathy knew growing up (think Jackie O with a platinum bob) made a version of this dish. That was in the '70s, when quiche was all the rage, but in our minds, it defies trend. She was a busy woman, so she skipped the crust and often baked the filling in individual ramekins in advance. When dinnertime rolled around, she'd warm a few in the oven and pull out some Italian bread for an effortless and popular meal.

Aside from blanching the broccoli, the quiche can be assembled in minutes. If you prefer to use frozen broccoli, there's no need to blanch it; just thaw and pat dry.

Preheat the oven to 350°F, with a rack in the middle position. Butter a 10-inch glass pie dish, then set aside.

Bring a large pot of water to a boil over high heat and season it generously with salt; it should taste like seawater. When it returns to a boil, add the broccoli and gently boil, stirring once or twice, until just crisp-tender, 1 to 2 minutes. Drain, rinse with cold water, then thoroughly pat dry and scatter over the bottom of the pie dish. Scatter the cheese evenly over top.

In a 1-quart measuring cup (see Tip) or medium bowl, whisk together the milk, cream, eggs, nutmeg, 1 teaspoon salt, and pepper to taste until smooth, then pour over the cheese. Bake until the custard is just set in the center, 35 to 40 minutes. (Don't worry if the center is a little trembly; it will cook a little more as it rests.) Let cool slightly before serving.

TIP For convenience, we use a 4-cup measuring cup to measure all of the ingredients for the quiche, ending with the custard, which we whisk right in the cup. First, measure the broccoli, then the cheese. Next, measure the 1 cup milk, add enough cream to reach 1⅔ cups, then add the eggs, nutmeg, salt, and pepper. Whisk together, then pour the custard into the dish.

EIGHT-LAYER NACHOS

Active **15 min**; Total **40 min**
Serves **8**

One 10-ounce bag frozen corn, thawed

2 tablespoons sunflower or olive oil, plus more for greasing

Kosher salt and pepper

One 15.5-ounce can refried black or pinto beans

½ teaspoon ground cumin

½ teaspoon finely grated lime zest

1 pint grape or cherry tomatoes, chopped (about 12 ounces)

½ cup finely chopped red onion

½ cup lightly packed cilantro leaves, chopped

3 tablespoons fresh lime juice

8 ounces sturdy corn tortilla chips (about 10 cups)

6 ounces sharp cheddar cheese, grated (about 1½ cups)

6 ounces Monterey Jack cheese, grated (about 1½ cups)

1 ripe avocado, peeled and chopped

Plain Greek yogurt, pickled jalapeño slices and hot sauce, for serving

Editor's Beer Choice Crisp, slightly malty ale: Anderson Valley Brewing Company Boont Amber Ale

"Each bite of nachos should be loaded with toppings," Brennan says. "There is nothing sadder than finding the bottom chips naked and neglected." So Brennan and Campion created these nachos that pile seven layers of toppings onto a single layer of tortilla chips.

1. Preheat the oven to 375°F. On a rimmed baking sheet, toss the corn with 1 tablespoon of the oil and season with salt and pepper. Spread the corn in a single layer and roast for about 15 minutes, tossing halfway through, until it begins to caramelize. Transfer the roasted corn to a bowl.

2. Meanwhile, in a small bowl, combine the refried beans with the cumin and lime zest. In a medium bowl, combine the tomatoes with the onion, cilantro, 2 tablespoons of the lime juice and the remaining 1 tablespoon of oil. Season the salsa with salt and pepper.

3. Lightly grease a large rimmed baking sheet and arrange the tortilla chips in a single layer on it. Top with the refried beans and cheese and bake for about 10 minutes, until the cheese is melted and beginning to brown.

4. Meanwhile, in a small bowl, mash the avocado with the remaining 1 tablespoon of lime juice; season the guacamole with salt and pepper.

5. Top the chips with the roasted corn, salsa, guacamole, yogurt and jalapeño slices. Serve with hot sauce on the side.

For more on Kathy Brennan & Caroline Campion
devilandegg.com
🅕 Keepers Cooks
🐦 @KeepersCooks

SCALLION
PANCAKES, P.58

FLOUR, TOO

Indispensable Recipes for the Café's Most Loved Sweets & Savories

BY **JOANNE CHANG**

BAKER Joanne Chang has that rare ability to master both sweet and savory foods. She owns four beloved Boston-area bakery-cafés all named Flour, but she also co-owns, with her husband, a pan-Asian restaurant, Myers+Chang. In her second book, she offers a simple yet deeply creative approach to many sweet and savory dishes. Take her scallion pancakes, for instance (pictured at left): She uses focaccia dough to make a perfectly light and airy version of her much-loved childhood snack. "It's the ultimate scallion pancake," she says of this staff and customer favorite at her restaurant. Chang is equally proud of her French toast (page 66): It's so good, she says, that she eats it plain.

Published by Chronicle Books, $35

SCALLION PANCAKES

Makes **3 large pancakes**

SPECIAL EQUIPMENT

Rimmed baking sheet, rolling pin

SCALLION PANCAKES

8 or 9 scallions, white and green parts, minced

¼ cup/60 ml sesame oil

1¼ teaspoons kosher salt

½ batch Flour Focaccia dough (page 60), or 1 pound/455 grams store-bought pizza dough

About 1½ cups/360 ml vegetable oil, for frying

SOY DIPPING SAUCE

3 tablespoons soy sauce

½ teaspoon Sriracha sauce

½ teaspoon sesame oil

1 tablespoon peeled and finely minced fresh ginger

1 teaspoon rice vinegar

1 tablespoon granulated sugar

1 scallion, white and green parts, minced

I grew up eating scallion pancakes in every shape and form. They were an easy snack that my mom bought frozen in the Asian grocery store, we made them carefully from scratch with my aunt when she visited from Taiwan, and we ordered them every time we went out for dinner at a Chinese restaurant. I learned quickly that there are huge variations in what you get, from a flaky, salty delicacy to a greasy, chewy, flavorless forgery.

When I opened Flour, it hit me that our popular focaccia dough would make an awesome fried dough, that guilty pleasure sold at outdoor fairs. And then I had a eureka moment and realized that the focaccia would make an even more awesome scallion pancake. The yeasted dough would fry up lighter and airier than the traditional dough, and I could combine the best of both worlds. At Myers+Chang, we use the focaccia dough from Flour, spread it with a mixture of sesame oil and scallions, shape it into rounds, and then fry the rounds to make the ultimate scallion pancake. They are a staff and customer favorite.

1. In a small bowl, mix together the scallions, sesame oil, and salt.

2. Cut the dough into thirds. On a well-floured work surface, roll out one portion of the dough into a thin 5-by-10-inch/12-by-25-cm rectangle. Repeat with the remaining two dough portions. Spread the scallion mixture evenly over the dough rectangles, leaving a ½-inch/12-mm border uncovered on all sides. Starting at a long side, roll up each rectangle jelly-roll style and pinch the seam with your fingers to seal. Spiral each cylinder into a tight coil and tuck the ends under the coil. Place in a warm area, cover loosely with plastic wrap, and let rest for about 2 hours to allow the dough to proof and relax. (At this point, the dough can be stored in an airtight container in the fridge overnight or in the freezer for up to 1 week; thaw in the fridge overnight before using.)

3. Line the baking sheet with a double layer of paper towels. Set aside.

4. On a generously floured work surface, press each coil into a flat circle, deflating any air pockets and squishing the scallions gently into the dough. With the rolling pin, slowly and carefully roll out each flattened circle into a 10-inch/25-cm round. Flour the dough and work surface as needed to prevent the dough from sticking. (It's okay if some of the scallion mixture comes out.) As you finish rolling each round, set it aside.

5. In a large skillet, heat the vegetable oil over medium-high heat until it is shimmering.

6. While the oil is heating, make the dipping sauce In a small bowl, whisk together the soy sauce, Sriracha sauce, sesame oil, ginger, vinegar, sugar, and scallion until the sugar has dissolved. Set aside. (The sauce can be made up to 1 week in advance and stored in the fridge in an airtight container.)

7. To check if the oil is ready, sprinkle a bit of flour into the skillet. If it sizzles on contact, the oil is ready. Carefully add one pancake to the hot oil and fry, turning once, for 1 to 2 minutes per side, or until golden. Transfer the pancake to the prepared baking sheet. Repeat with the remaining pancakes, always allowing the oil to return to temperature before adding the next one.

8. Cut the pancakes into quarters, arrange on a platter, and serve hot with the dipping sauce.

FLOUR FOCACCIA

Makes **about 2¼ pounds/1 kg dough,** enough for **1 large sandwich loaf** (for 4 or 5 sandwiches), **10 pockets,** or **2 large pizzas**

SPECIAL EQUIPMENT

Stand mixer with dough hook attachment, rimmed baking sheet

FOCACCIA

- 1 teaspoon active dry yeast, or 0.2 ounce/5 grams fresh cake yeast
- 3 cups/420 grams all-purpose flour, plus more for dusting
- 1 cup/150 grams bread flour
- 5 teaspoons granulated sugar
- 2 teaspoons kosher salt
- ½ cup/120 ml olive oil
- Small handful of cornmeal for sprinkling on the baking sheet

This is the recipe for our legendary sandwich bread. When I opened Flour, I had originally planned on buying bread from a wholesale bread bakery and using a different bread for each sandwich: *ciabatta* for this, sourdough for that, *pain de mie* for those, and so on. I planned on making one sandwich bread myself–a house-made focaccia–that we would use for only one of our sandwiches. Our opening chef, Chris, loved this focaccia so much he asked if we could make enough of it each day for all of the sandwiches. That wasn't in my game plan at all, but one of the first things you learn when opening a business is how to change your plans fast. We made dozens of loaves that first opening day, and we've never looked back. I honestly think it's a key to the popularity of our sandwiches. It's certainly easier to buy a loaf of bread to make the sandwiches in this book, but I promise you that if you make this bread you'll be rewarded with the best sandwiches you've ever had. We use this versatile dough for our pockets, our egg sandwiches, and our pizzas, as well.

1. In the bowl of the stand mixer, combine 1½ cups/360 ml tepid water and the yeast and let sit for 20 to 30 seconds to allow the yeast to dissolve and activate. Dump the all-purpose flour, bread flour, sugar, and salt into the water. Carefully turn the mixer on to low speed and mix for about 10 seconds. (To prevent the flour from flying out of the bowl, turn the mixer on and off several times until the flour is mixed into the liquid, and then keep it on low speed.) When the dough is still shaggy looking, drizzle in the olive oil, aiming it along the side of the bowl to keep it from splashing and making a mess.

2. With the mixer still on low speed, knead the dough for 4 to 5 minutes, or until it is smooth and supple. The dough should be somewhat sticky but still smooth and have an elastic, stretchy texture. (If it is much stiffer than this, mix in 1 to 2 tablespoons water; if it is much looser than this, mix in 2 to 3 tablespoons all-purpose flour.)

3. Lightly oil a large bowl. Transfer the dough to the oiled bowl, cover with an oiled piece of plastic wrap or a damp lint-free cloth, and place in a draft-free, warm (78° to 82°F/25° to 27°C is ideal) area for 2 to 3 hours. An area near the stove or in the oven with only the oven light on is good. The dough should rise until it is about double in bulk. (This is called proofing the dough.)

4. Sprinkle the baking sheet with the cornmeal and set aside. Once the dough has risen, flour your hands and the work surface and turn the dough out onto the work surface. Press the dough into an 8-inch/20-cm square and fold the top edge of the square down to the center of the dough. Fold the bottom of the square up to the center of the dough and press the seam firmly with your fingers. Now fold the right side of the square into the center and the left side into the center, and again press the seam firmly. Turn the dough over, seam-side down, and shape the dough with a tucking motion so that it is about 6 inches/15 cm square. Transfer the dough to the prepared baking sheet, generously flour the top of the dough, and then cover the dough loosely but completely with a damp lint-free cloth or a piece of plastic wrap. Place in a warm area (78° to 82°F/25° to 27°C) for another hour or so, or until the dough rises a bit and gets puffy and pillowy. (This is proofing, again.) If making scallion pancakes, hot pockets, egg sandwiches, or turkey burgers: Split the dough in half and reserve half of the dough for another use. Proceed with the desired recipe as directed. These recipes can be easily doubled, in which case use the entire batch of dough and proceed as directed.

5. Preheat the oven to 400°F/200°C, and place a rack in the center of the oven.

6. When the dough is ready, remove the cloth or plastic wrap. Using all ten fingers, press and poke and elongate the dough three or four times along its length so that you press and stretch it into an almost-square log that is about 10 inches/25 cm long, 8 inches/20 cm wide, and about 2 inches/5 cm tall. Bake for 35 to 45 minutes, or until completely golden brown on the top and bottom. Lift the loaf and make sure the underside is browned before pulling it out of the oven, or you will end up with a soggy loaf. Let cool on the pan on a wire rack for about 30 minutes, or until cool enough to handle, then cut into slices ¾ inch/2 cm thick for sandwiches. The focaccia loaf will keep in a closed paper bag at room temperature for up to 3 days, or tightly wrapped in two layers of plastic wrap in the freezer for up to 2 weeks. If using day-old bread kept at room temperature, I suggest toasting it in a toaster to refresh it. If using bread that has been previously frozen, thaw it at room temperature for 3 to 4 hours and then refresh it in a 300°F/150°C oven for about 5 minutes.

MAMA CHANG'S HOT & SOUR

Makes **about 1¾ quarts/1.75 liters**
Serves **4**

SPECIAL EQUIPMENT

Large saucepan

HOT & SOUR

2 **tablespoons vegetable oil**

1 **garlic clove, smashed and minced**

1 **tablespoon peeled and minced fresh ginger**

4 **scallions, white and green parts, minced, plus 2 tablespoons chopped for garnish**

8 **ounces/225 grams ground pork**

4 **cups/960 ml chicken stock**

One **1-pound/455-gram block soft or firm tofu (not silken and not extra-firm), cut into ½-inch/12-mm cubes**

4 or 5 **medium button mushrooms, wiped clean and thinly sliced**

1 **teaspoon granulated sugar**

⅔ **cup/160 ml rice vinegar**

3 **tablespoons soy sauce**

1 **teaspoon freshly ground black pepper**

1 **tablespoon sesame oil, plus 2 teaspoons for garnish**

1 **tablespoon Sriracha sauce**

2 **large eggs**

White pepper for garnish

Here are all of the bright and peppery flavors of the hot-and-sour soup you get at a restaurant with none of the glop. Ground pork is not traditional, but it makes the preparation of this soup ultraquick. Wood ear mushrooms, sometimes labeled "tree fungus" (now there's an appetizing name), are a standard addition, but they can be hard to find unless you live near an Asian grocery store. I substitute easy-to-find button mushrooms, which don't have the same crunch but add a nice earthy flavor. Egg, not flavorless cornstarch, acts as the thickener, allowing the flavors of pork, sesame, vinegar, and pepper to come shining through. My mom used to whip this up as a fast lunch for my brother and me, and I have taught it to the Flour chefs, so they now offer it as a daily soup special. It always sells out, and Mom is thrilled to be part of the Flour menu.

1. In the saucepan, heat the vegetable oil over medium-high heat until hot. Add the garlic, ginger, scallions, and ground pork and cook, stirring occasionally, for about 1 minute. Break up the pork into smaller pieces but don't worry about breaking it down completely. Add the stock and bring to a simmer.

2. Add the tofu, mushrooms, sugar, vinegar, soy sauce, black pepper, sesame oil, and Sriracha sauce and bring the soup back to a simmer over medium-high heat. (Taste the soup. If you want it hotter, add more Sriracha sauce; if you want it more sour, add more vinegar.)

3. In a small bowl, whisk the eggs until blended. With the soup at a steady simmer, slowly whisk in the eggs so they form strands. Bring the soup back to a simmer. Divide the soup among four bowls and garnish each with a little sesame oil, scallion, and white pepper. Serve immediately. The soup can be stored in an airtight container in the fridge for up to 3 days.

This is a more
wholesome
version of the
takeout staple.

BUTTERMILK-FRIED CHICKEN

Serves **4**

SPECIAL EQUIPMENT

Sharp boning knife; 9-by-13-inch/23-by-33-cm baking dish or other shallow container; large, deep, heavy skillet; deep-fry thermometer; rimmed baking sheet

BUTTERMILK-FRIED CHICKEN

One 4- to 4½-pound/1.8- to 2-kg whole chicken

1 **teaspoon paprika**

1 **teaspoon freshly ground black pepper**

1 **teaspoon garlic powder**

1 **teaspoon onion powder**

1 **teaspoon dry mustard**

2 **cups/480 ml nonfat buttermilk**

3 **fresh tarragon sprigs, roughly chopped**

1 **medium onion, peeled and cut into ½-inch/12-mm pieces**

1 **tablespoon kosher salt**

2 **cups/280 grams all-purpose flour**

4 **cups/960 ml vegetable oil, for frying**

Editor's Wine Choice
Robust, juicy rosé:
2013 Crios Rosé of Malbec

Within Flour, Chef Aniceto [Sousa] is known among the other chefs for having the most adventurous and diverse specials. His time at two four-star French restaurants, a Middle Eastern bakery-café, and a nose-to-tail farm-driven bistro, along with his own perpetual food curiosity, have led him to introduce all of us to ingredients and techniques that we'd never have known about without him. So imagine my surprise when he came up with a dinner special that was as American as apple pie. Fried chicken, done right, is a rare treat. He bemoans the fact that because all of our dinner specials are made in advance to be reheated at home, customers don't get to enjoy chicken straight out of the fryer. It's a testament to how delicious this chicken is that it's just as good (some would say better) cold as it is hot. Now you can try it yourself. Note that the chicken has to marinate for a day in the buttermilk, so you need to start this recipe a day in advance.

1. The day before you plan to serve the chicken, cut the chicken into ten pieces. First, take a drumstick and pull it away from the body. Feel for the thigh joint where the thigh meets the body and cut at the joint—if you stick a boning knife along the joint you'll feel the joint where it's soft (versus the bone where it's hard) and you'll be able to cut through. Repeat on the other side. Separate the thighs from the drumsticks again by cutting at the joint. Set aside. Press the body of the chicken (breast-side up) flat against your cutting board. You'll hear the back bones crack a bit. Lift up the body and slice down the middle of the chicken to separate the bony back from the breast. (Reserve the back bones to make stock.) Cut the breast in half right down the middle of the bone; you may have to switch to a larger chef's knife to cut through the bone. Cut the wings off the breast, including some of the breast meat so that the wings have some good meat to them. Set the wings aside. Cut the remaining breast halves crosswise in half again. You will now have ten pieces of chicken all approximately the same size. Arrange the chicken pieces in a single layer in the baking dish.

2. In a small container, mix together the paprika, pepper, garlic powder, onion powder, and dry mustard until blended.

3. Pour the buttermilk into a small bowl. Add about half of the spice mixture and whisk it into the buttermilk. Stir in the tarragon, onion, and salt. Pour the marinade over the chicken pieces, cover with plastic wrap, and refrigerate overnight.

4. The next day, in a medium bowl, whisk together the remaining spice mixture and the flour, then transfer the mixture to a pie pan or other flat, shallow pan with a rim. Remove the chicken pieces from the buttermilk, shaking them to remove any excess liquid. Dredge each piece on both sides in the flour mixture and shake off any excess. Set aside on a large platter or plate.

5. Pour the vegetable oil into the skillet and heat to 375°F/190°C on the deep-fry thermometer. While the oil heats, line the baking sheet with paper towels and set aside. Using kitchen tongs or a slotted spoon, carefully place all of the dark meat (these pieces will need to cook a bit longer) into the skillet. The temperature will drop to between 350° and 325°F/180° and 165°C. Cook on both sides, turning once or twice, for 12 to 15 minutes, or until the chicken is browned and cooked through. Transfer to the prepared baking sheet to drain. Repeat with the white meat, which will take 8 to 10 minutes. The chicken can be cooked in advance, covered and stored in the fridge, and reheated in a 350°F/180°C oven for about 10 minutes to restore crunch before serving.

FABULOUS FRENCH TOAST

Makes **6 slices**

SPECIAL EQUIPMENT

Large, flat nonstick skillet; rimmed baking sheet; sieve or sifter

FRENCH TOAST

6 **large eggs**

²⁄₃ **cup/135 grams vanilla sugar**

½ **teaspoon kosher salt**

2 **cups/480 ml half-and-half**

6 **slices country-style sourdough bread, 1 inch/2.5 cm thick, preferably 1 day old**

3 to 4 tablespoons unsalted butter, plus extra for serving

2 **tablespoons confectioners' sugar for garnish**

Maple syrup for serving

The most important thing about making great French toast is starting with great bread. It doesn't have to be fresh (in fact–the older, the better, because the bread will soak up more custard when it's dried out and stale), but it should be a hearty country-style loaf. The bread spends the night in the fridge in a simple custard bath: vanilla sugar, eggs, half-and-half. By the time you cook it it's so filled with custard that it almost seems to soufflé. You start it in a skillet to give it a lovely caramelized crust on the outside and then you finish it in the oven. It's so deliciously airy and eggy that I usually eat it as is, sans butter and syrup, but for a special breakfast treat do it up right with all of the trimmings.

1. Into a small bowl, crack the eggs and slowly whisk in the sugar and salt. Whisk in the half-and half. Place the bread in a single layer in a shallow container and pour the egg mixture over the bread. Turn the bread over to coat both sides and cover with plastic wrap. Refrigerate overnight.

2. The next morning, turn the bread over again. Preheat the oven to 350°F/180°C, and place a rack in the center of the oven.

3. In the skillet, heat about 1 tablespoon of the butter over medium-high heat. Sprinkle a few drops of water into the pan; if the water sizzles on contact, the pan is ready. Place two slices of French toast in the pan and cook on one side for 2 to 3 minutes, or until golden brown. Flip them over and cook for 2 to 3 minutes longer, or until the second side is golden brown. Remove from the heat and place on the baking sheet. Repeat with the remaining French toast in two batches, adding 1 tablespoon or so of the butter to the skillet each time.

4. When all the slices have been fried, place the baking sheet in the oven for 8 to 10 minutes to finish the cooking. When the French toast is done, the insides will be custardy and soft but no longer soggy and wet. Using the sieve, dust the tops with the confectioners' sugar. Serve immediately with butter and maple syrup.

RASPBERRY-HONEY FROZEN YOGURT

Total **40 min plus 3 hr freezing**
Makes **1 quart**

1¼ cups plain whole-milk Greek
  yogurt

 1 pound (about 2 pints) fresh
  or frozen raspberries

⅔ cup honey

 1 tablespoon fresh lemon juice

 1 tablespoon pure vanilla extract

⅛ teaspoon kosher salt

Chang loves the pure raspberry flavor in this easy recipe. In fact, when her husband first tried it, he declared that it tasted exactly like a bowl of fresh raspberries.

1. In a food processor, combine all of the ingredients and puree until smooth. Strain three-quarters of the yogurt mixture through a sieve into a medium bowl; discard the seeds. Stir in the remaining yogurt mixture.

2. Pour the yogurt mixture into an ice cream maker and freeze according to the manufacturer's instructions. Scrape the yogurt into an airtight container and freeze for at least 3 hours, until the yogurt is firm.

3. Remove the frozen yogurt from the freezer 10 minutes before serving to let it soften slightly.

MAKE AHEAD The yogurt can be frozen for up to 1 week.

**For more on
Joanne Chang**
Flour Bakery + Cafe
@jbchang

THE CHEFS COLLABORATIVE COOKBOOK

Local, Sustainable, Delicious Recipes from America's Great Chefs

BY **CHEFS COLLABORATIVE** & **ELLEN JACKSON**

WITH a primer on GMOs, a breakdown of organic food costs and a guide to buying responsibly raised meat, this book has a wealth of practical information. But the recipes are what set it apart. Chefs Collaborative–a nonprofit organization devoted to developing and promoting sustainable food practices–solicited dishes from 116 North American chefs with wide-ranging backgrounds and specialties. The results cover a remarkable amount of territory, from a pork and hominy stew (page 70) by Southern legend Robert Stehling to a light, savory, miso-marinated (and ocean-friendly) sablefish (page 72) from California wine country chef John Ash. All told, the recipes form an eclectic collection that supports an admirable cause.

Published by The Taunton Press, $40

PORK SHOULDER & HOMINY STEW

Robert Stehling, Hominy Grill, Charleston, South Carolina

Serves **6**

2 tablespoons bacon fat

One 2½-pound boneless pork shoulder roast, cut into 1½-inch pieces

2 medium onions, diced (about 2 cups)

2 stalks celery, diced (½ cup)

2 cloves garlic, finely minced

1 green bell pepper, diced (1 cup)

3 cups pork or chicken stock

2 bay leaves

1 teaspoon dried thyme

1 teaspoon dried basil

Pinch of crushed red pepper flakes

1 teaspoon freshly ground black pepper

1½ teaspoons kosher salt; more as needed

4 cups whole hominy, cooked, with 1 cup of the cooking liquid reserved (or two 14-ounce cans, rinsed and drained)

¼ cup coarsely chopped fresh flat-leaf parsley

¼ cup sliced scallions, white and green parts

Editor's Wine Choice
Lively, raspberry-rich Spanish Garnacha: 2012 Evodia

The pork shoulder makes up 25 percent of a hog's carcass weight and is typically divided into a top portion—the Boston butt—and bottom portion—the picnic roast. These well-exercised muscles are rich, flavorful, and inexpensive. When braised or cooked with moist heat, these large cuts of meat taste better over time.

This hearty stew is complete when garnished with fried apple and onion rings; add a poached egg on top and serve for brunch.

Heat 1 tablespoon of the bacon fat in a large Dutch oven or braising pot (5 quarts is a good size) over medium-high heat. Brown the pork on all sides, turning the pieces with tongs as you go. Remove the meat and put it on a large plate to collect any juice that it releases.

Add the remaining 1 tablespoon of bacon fat and the onions to the pot and cook over medium-high heat, stirring frequently, until the onions begin to brown slightly. Add the celery and continue to cook and stir until almost tender, then add the garlic. Cook the garlic for 2 minutes, add the bell peppers, and continue cooking until they are wilted, about 5 minutes.

Increase the heat to high and add the pork to the pot with the stock, bay leaves, thyme, basil, red pepper flakes, black pepper, salt, and cooked hominy. Bring the mixture to a simmer and cook over low heat until the pork becomes tender, about 2 hours. Add a reserved cup of hominy cooking liquid if necessary.

Season to taste with salt, if necessary (the salt content in canned hominy varies). Stir in the parsley and scallions just before serving.

MISO-MARINATED SABLEFISH

John Ash, Santa Rosa, California

Serves **6**

¼ cup mirin

¼ cup sake wine

½ cup plus 2 tablespoons white *shiro* miso

⅓ cup granulated sugar

6 sablefish fillets, skin on, 6 to 7 ounces each

3 tablespoons canola or grapeseed oil

Pickled sushi ginger, for garnish

Sesame seeds, toasted, for garnish

Daikon sprouts, for garnish

Editor's Wine Choice Minerally, full-bodied Alsace Pinot Blanc: 2012 Domaine Ostertag Barriques

Sablefish, which is also known as black cod or butterfish, is a sustainably caught fish that comes mostly from Alaska, though it is also abundant in parts of the Pacific Northwest. Marinating it in miso, the umami-rich paste made with soybeans, rice, and/or barley, is a traditional preparation, but the marinade is also wonderful slathered on other kinds of fish, chicken, and pork. Serve the sablefish with sweet pickled sushi ginger, toasted sesame seeds, and daikon sprouts.

Combine the mirin and sake in a small saucepan and bring to a boil. Whisk in the miso until smooth, then add the sugar and cook over medium heat, stirring constantly, until the sugar has dissolved. Transfer the marinade to a bowl and cool.

Pat the fillets thoroughly with paper towels and generously coat with marinade on both sides. Place in a nonreactive bowl or dish with any remaining marinade, cover tightly with plastic wrap, and refrigerate for at least 8 hours or overnight.

Heat the oven to 400°F. Warm the oil over medium-high heat in an ovenproof sauté pan large enough to hold the fish in one layer. When the oil is hot, scrape the excess marinade off the fish and cook the fish until lightly browned on one side, about 2 minutes. Turn the fish and place the pan in the oven until the fish is cooked through and flaky, about 8 minutes. Serve on warm plates topped with the garnishes.

Sablefish has a silky texture similar to that of Chilean sea bass.

AMISH HAND-PULLED CHICKEN SALAD

Todd Gray, Equinox, Washington, DC

Serves **6**

**One 2½-pound roasted chicken,
    cooled**

  1 **small red onion, finely chopped**

  2 **ribs celery, finely chopped**

  1 **cup mayonnaise**

  1 **cup cashews, lightly toasted and
       coarsely chopped**

⅓ **cup dried cherries, coarsely
       chopped**

1½ **tablespoons coarsely chopped
       fresh tarragon**

**Kosher salt and freshly ground
    black pepper**

Editor's Wine Choice Berry-
scented, lightly floral Provençal
rosé: 2013 AIX

A whole roast chicken is the beginning of many good things, with leftovers somewhere close to the top of the list. If you don't have enough meat left over, roast a chicken just for this salad—it's worthy of its own bird. The combination of textures and flavors in the recipe is welcome as the weather turns cooler. After you pull the meat from the carcass, toss the bones in a pot with a coarsely chopped onion, a carrot, and some celery; cover with water, add a bay leaf, a few peppercorns, and some parsley stems, and simmer on low for a flavorful broth.

After removing the skin from the roast chicken, pull the meat from the breast and legs, tearing it into bite-size pieces. You should have about 4 cups of chicken. Add it to a large bowl with the onions and celery and toss until the ingredients are evenly distributed. Fold in the mayonnaise, stirring to coat all of the chicken pieces. Add the cashews, cherries, and tarragon and season to taste with salt and black pepper. Allow the salad to chill for 30 minutes before serving.

VANILLA CARROT CREAM TART

Phoebe Lawless, Scratch Baking, Durham, North Carolina

Serves **8 to 10**

FOR THE TART DOUGH

- ½ cup confectioners' sugar
- ½ teaspoon kosher salt
- 6 tablespoons (¾ stick) cold unsalted butter, diced into ½-inch cubes
- 1 large egg
- 1 tablespoon heavy cream
- 1½ cups unbleached all-purpose flour

FOR THE FILLING

- 3 medium carrots, peeled and sliced into ½-inch-thick coins (about 1½ cups)
- ⅔ cup heavy cream
- ½ vanilla bean
- 2 large eggs
- 1 large egg yolk
- ⅓ cup granulated sugar
- Pinch of kosher salt
- 1 cup buttermilk

The carrots that begin showing up at farmer's markets in early spring—especially the smaller heirloom varieties—add surprising natural sweetness to custard fillings like this one. This tart is a lovely way to make use of local produce at a time of year when rhubarb and other harbingers of spring have yet to make an appearance.

Combine the confectioners' sugar, salt, and butter in the bowl of a food processor. Pulse several times until the mixture resembles small pebbles. Add the egg and heavy cream and pulse again. Add the flour all at once and pulse in bursts until the dough begins to come together. Scrape the dough out onto a clean, lightly floured work surface.

Working quickly and using the heel of your hand or a dough scraper, smear the dough across the floured surface a little at a time to incorporate the butter. This French technique, called *fraisage*, is the key to a tender, flaky crust.

When all of the dough has been smeared, gather it together in a mass and gently form a flat disk that's 1½ inches thick. Wrap tightly with plastic wrap and chill for at least 1 hour or freeze for up to 1 month. If using the dough right away, after an hour, remove the dough from the refrigerator and allow it to sit out for 10 to 15 minutes, to make it easier to roll.

On a lightly floured work surface, roll the dough into a 14- to 15-inch circle that's ¼ inch thick. Fold the dough in half and carefully lay it in a 10-inch tart pan with a false bottom and fluted edges. Lightly press the dough into the corners and fold the outer edge of the pastry into the sides, pressing to create an even wall that extends just beyond the top of the pan. Pinch off excess pastry and reserve the extra dough. Prick the shell with a fork and freeze for at least 15 minutes.

To make the filling, combine the carrots and heavy cream in a small nonreactive saucepan. Split the vanilla bean half, scrape the seeds, and add them to the pan along with the pod. Simmer the mixture, covered, over low heat until the carrots are soft, about 20 minutes. Cool completely, remove the vanilla pod, and purée with an immersion blender or in a regular blender until very smooth.

continued on page 76

VANILLA CARROT
CREAM TART *continued*

In a medium bowl, whisk the eggs, egg yolk, sugar, and salt until well combined. Add the cool carrot purée and buttermilk. This mixture can be made and refrigerated 2 days ahead.

Heat the oven to 325°F. Bake the tart shell for 15 to 20 minutes, or until the bottom is lightly golden. If the dough begins to bubble up, use a clean dry towel to gently press it down.

Pour the filling into the partially baked shell and then bake for 30 to 40 minutes, or until the edges puff slightly. The tart will be jiggly in the center and appear to be underbaked—this is okay. Cool at room temperature for 30 minutes, then chill until set, about 2 hours.

Remove the tart from the pan and serve at room temperature the day it is baked or chilled the following day.

For more on Chefs Collaborative
chefscollaborative.org
Chefs Collaborative
@chefscollab

This is a lovely
alternative to
pumpkin pie for
Thanksgiving.

"L.A. is a huge place, and sometimes the glare of stereotypes and television screens blinds visitors to its true character." –Roy Choi, *here with ribs from Phillips Bar-B-Que in L.A.'s Leimert Park*

L.A. SON

My Life, My City, My Food

BY **ROY CHOI** WITH
TIEN NGUYEN & **NATASHA PHAN**

HELLO. I'm Roy. Get in." So begins this vivid memoir from Roy Choi, chef and founder of the Kogi BBQ taco truck empire. What follows is a journey that goes deep into off-the-strip Los Angeles and beyond: Koreatown, the barrios of East L.A. and Little Saigon. And since food is an inextricable part of Korean-born Choi's coming-of-age in L.A., his memoir is also a feast, beginning with kimchi ("A car needs gas; as a kid, I needed kimchi") and spanning multiple cuisines. Choi's deeply flavorful carne asada (page 86) is his version of L.A.'s most common street food, and his ketchup fried rice (page 84) is a shout-out to "trashy" comfort food. Smart recipes, like a sharply tangy, generously dressed Caesar salad (page 82), also reveal Choi's talents as a chef, not just a street-and-stoner-food king.

Published by Ecco, $30

KOREAN-STYLE BRAISED SHORT RIB STEW

Serves **4 to 6**

SAUCE

½ cup chopped scallions

1½ cups soy sauce

¼ cup chopped peeled fresh ginger

½ white or yellow onion, peeled

½ cup garlic cloves, peeled

½ cup sugar

½ cup mirin

½ cup fresh orange juice

½ cup apple juice

4 cups water

4 pounds short ribs, soaked in cold water in the refrigerator overnight

VEGETABLES

8 ounces shiitake mushrooms, stems discarded

1 cup jarred chestnuts, peeled

1 cub cubed taro

1 cup carrots in large dice

1 cup cubed butternut squash

Editor's Wine Choice
Generously fruit-forward
Spanish red: 2012 Zestos
Garnacha Old Vines

This is that meal from home that every Korean kid says his or her mom does best, the dish that gets packed in CorningWare and taken to parties, the dish that creates some serious lines in the sand over friendship and heated arguments over who seems to know it better or "owns" the best-of-the-best title for it. I don't know whose mom does it best, so try mine.

In a blender or food processor, combine all the ingredients for the sauce except 3 cups of water and puree. Add the pureed sauce, plus the remaining 3 cups water, to a large pot, stir, and bring to a boil.

Meanwhile, remove the soaked ribs from the fridge, drain, rinse, and drain again. Score the ribs across the top of the meat in diagonal slashes. When the sauce has come to a boil, add the ribs. Lower the heat to a simmer and cover the pot.

Let the sauce and the ribs cook for at least 2 hours over low heat, then add the vegetables, replace the cover, and simmer for another 30 minutes or so, until the meat is tender and the vegetables are cooked but retain their integrity.

Serve with rice.

CAESAR SALAD

Serves **8**

DRESSING

- 3 tablespoons chopped garlic
- 2 tablespoons chopped anchovies
- 3 large egg yolks
- ¾ teaspoon dry mustard
- 1½ teaspoons freshly ground black pepper
- 1 cup plus 1 tablespoon extra-virgin olive oil
- ½ cup fresh lemon juice
- 2 cups mayonnaise
- 2½ tablespoons Worcestershire sauce
- 2 tablespoons pureed onion
- 1 tablespoon water

Good pinch of salt

SALAD

- 8 romaine hearts, separated into leaves
- 2 cups shaved Parmesan cheese
- 1 lemon

Cracked black pepper

Yes, it's everywhere, but this one is really good, I swear. Don't omit the shaved Parmesan–the salad won't taste complete until you add it at the end.

Leftover dressing will keep in your refrigerator for up to 5 days.

Combine all the dressing ingredients in a blender and puree.

Toss the romaine leaves with the dressing, coating with liberal intent.

Plate the leaves and shower each plate with Parmesan, a light squeeze of lemon, and big twists of cracked black pepper from the peppermill.

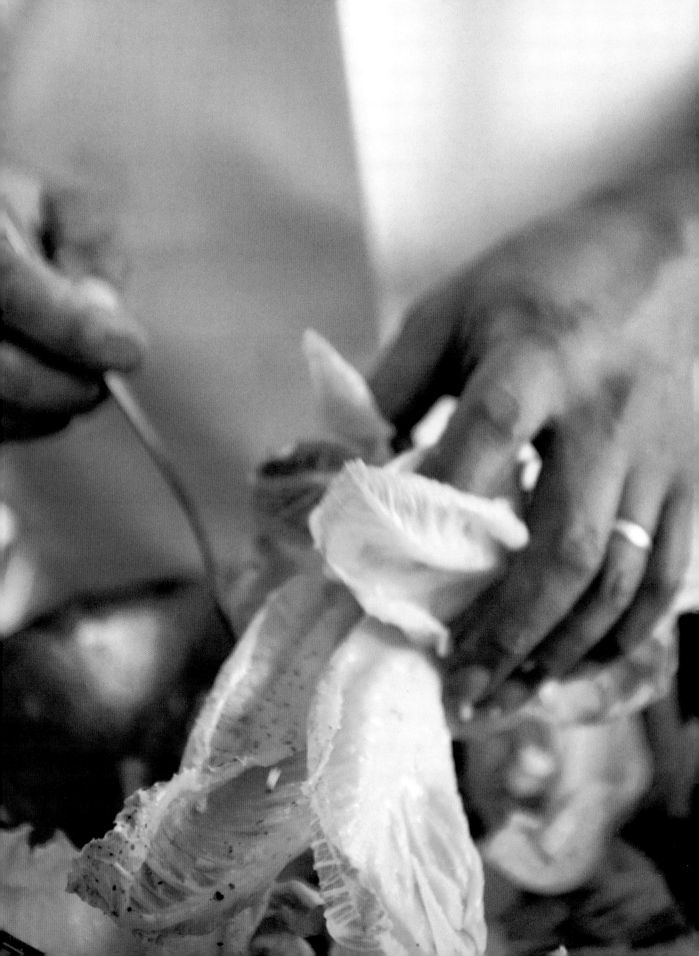

KETCHUP FRIED RICE

Serves **4 to 6**

3 tablespoons vegetable oil

1 tablespoon minced scallions

1 tablespoon minced carrot

1 teaspoon minced garlic

1 tablespoon minced kimchi

2 cups day-old cooked rice

3 tablespoons ketchup

1 egg

¾ teaspoon roasted and crushed sesame seeds

Editor's Beer Choice Ice-cold beer: Dos Equis Lager

Ain't nothing more ghetto than ketchup fried rice. This is a fiend's meal. It's like crackers and aerosol cheese spread. It's like sugar on some white bread or frozen burritos.

Heat a large pan or a wok over high heat and add the oil. Throw in all the vegetables and the kimchi and sauté for a minute or so, until you start to see a little color on the veggies. Transfer the veggies to a bowl and return the pan to the stove.

Add a touch more oil to the pan and add the rice, stirring it around occasionally. Cook the rice until it gets a bit crispy, then add the vegetables to the rice and mix for a minute or two. Add the ketchup and mix everything around until the rice fully absorbs the ketchup. Remove from the heat and put a small pan over the flame. Fry your egg however you like.

Serve yourself a bowl of the rice and top with the fried egg and a sprinkle of sesame seeds.

The more fermented the kimchi, the more intense the flavor.

CARNE ASADA

Serves **4**

MARINADE

- ¼ **cup garlic cloves, peeled**
- ¼ **onion, peeled**
- ¼ **cup chopped scallions**
- ¼ **cup ancho chile powder**
- 1 **tablespoon freshly ground black pepper**
- 2 **jalapeño peppers**
- ½ **bunch fresh cilantro**
- ¾ **cup Budweiser or any other beer you got in the fridge**
- **Juice and grated zest of 1 orange**
- **Juice and grated zest of 2 limes**
- ½ **kiwifruit, peeled**
- ¼ **cup mirin**
- **Good pinch of kosher salt**
- **Good pinch of sugar**

- 1 **pound skirt steak**
- **Canola oil, for oiling the grill**

Editor's Beer Choice
Slightly malty amber
ale: Lagunitas Censored
Copper Ale

There are few foods more emblematic of Los Angeles than carne asada. In fact, the phrase has become so recognizable that you don't even have to translate it to English: just say it out loud, and most people will know it's marinated beef, thinly sliced and grilled to a char on a sunny Cali picnic day. I have heavy roots with carne asada: I grew up around it in Koreatown and ate it almost every day as a lowrider. I love that it's a wet marinade but somehow dries the meat just right. Whenever you eat carne asada, it feels like L.A. Wash it down with some fresh horchata. *Orale, carnal.*

Combine all the ingredients for the marinade in a blender or food processor and puree.

Rub the marinade all over the steak and marinate the meat in the refrigerator, covered, for at least an hour and up to 2 days.

When you're ready to grill, heat the grill to medium heat, brush with oil, and cook the steak for 10 minutes, until it's nice and charred on the outside and medium on the inside.

Rest the meat for 5 to 10 minutes; then eat.

SPICY KOREAN PORK BBQ

Total **45 min plus 12 hr marinating**
Serves **4 to 6**

SPICY MARINADE

**1½ cups Galbi Marinade
   (recipe follows)**

½ cup *gochujang*

**2 tablespoons *gochugaru*
   (Korean chile powder)**

1 jalapeño, chopped

2 tablespoons sugar

4 garlic cloves, crushed

PORK

**3 pounds thinly sliced pork
   shoulder (about ½ inch thick)**

Canola oil, for oiling the grill

Editor's Beer Choice Refreshing
Mexican lager: Pacifico

Total **15 min**
Makes **about 1½ cups**

½ cup soy sauce

⅓ cup sugar

¼ cup maple syrup

½ small onion, quartered

½ scallion, chopped

**3 garlic cloves,
   crushed**

¼ kiwi, peeled and chopped

**¼ Asian pear, peeled
   and chopped**

Choi's recipe is the ultimate version of Korean BBQ: super-tender pork coated with a sweet, spicy and savory glaze. He adds maple syrup to the *gochujang* (Korean chile paste) marinade, so the edges of the pork get charred and caramelized.

1. Make the spicy marinade In a blender, combine all of the ingredients and puree until smooth.

2. Prepare the pork In a large bowl, combine the pork with 1½ cups of the spicy marinade. Massage the pork to coat, cover and refrigerate for at least 12 hours and up to 24 hours.

3. Light a grill and oil the grate. Remove the pork from the marinade; discard the marinade. Grill the pork over medium heat, turning, until nicely charred and cooked through, 6 to 8 minutes. Transfer the pork to a platter and serve hot.

Galbi Marinade

You can use this marinade on thinly sliced bone-in short ribs (*galbi* or flanken-style). Marinate the ribs overnight in the refrigerator, then bring to room temperature before grilling until well browned and charred in spots.

In a blender, combine all of the ingredients and puree until smooth. Use right away or refrigerate for up to 3 days.

For more on Roy Choi
ridingshotgunla.com
f Riding Shotgun
🐦 @RidingShotgunLA

BEET GREENS STRATA, P.90

ROOT-TO-STALK COOKING

The Art of Using the Whole Vegetable

BY **TARA DUGGAN**

THE broccoli salad itself is convincing (page 92). Composed of broccoli stalks shaved paper-thin and dressed with lime juice and salty Cotija cheese, it's a brilliant use of what otherwise might have been tossed, and part of the delicious campaign against waste that Tara Duggan wages in her instructive new book. Duggan, a San Francisco–based food writer, urges us to take our enthusiasm for farmers' markets and CSAs a step further by cooking with every last bit of in-season vegetables. There are relishes and chutneys, and even an apple peel bourbon, but also hearty main courses, like a fennel-braised pork roast (page 91) that uses fennel stalks and fronds, not just bulbs–in other words, the surprisingly tasty parts that ordinarily get scrapped.

Published by Ten Speed Press, $22

BEET GREENS STRATA

Serves **4**

1 teaspoon olive oil, plus more for greasing the pan

Greens from 1 bunch beets, washed

½ cup finely minced onion, leek, or green onion (white and light green parts)

Kosher salt and freshly ground pepper

1 cup milk

3 large eggs

3 cups bread such as walnut bread, artisan whole wheat, or country bread (preferably day-old or stale), cut into 1-inch cubes

1 cup shredded Gruyère cheese

Author's Note If you like, you can add 1 cup cooked and crumbled sausage to the bread when you toss it with the greens.

Editor's Wine Choice
Lively, citrusy Prosecco:
NV Mionetto Brut

Like a savory bread pudding, a strata is the perfect brunch dish because you can make it in the evening, perhaps after using the beets in another dish at dinner. You let the bread soak up the custard overnight, and then bake it in the morning. (It's also a fine way to use up extra bread.) On the small side, this recipe uses the greens from one bunch of beets. If you'd like to double it for a larger crowd, just augment with chard or other greens.

Grease an 8-by-8-inch baking dish with olive oil.

As you would with chard, remove the stems from the beet leaves. Thinly slice the stems and cut the leaves into ribbons. Place a large frying pan over medium heat and add the olive oil. Add the onion and beet stems and cook, stirring frequently, until partly tender, about 4 minutes. Add the leaves a few handfuls at a time and cook until wilted, 1 to 2 minutes. Add a splash of water, cover, and cook until the greens and stems are tender, 2 to 3 minutes. Season with salt and pepper and set aside to cool slightly.

In a medium bowl, combine the milk, eggs, ½ teaspoon salt, and several grindings of pepper. Whisk until smooth.

In a medium bowl, toss the bread with the greens and half of the cheese. Spread the mixture in the prepared pan. Slowly pour the egg mixture over so that the bread is evenly coated. Poke down any pieces of bread that can be further nestled in the custard, then top with the remaining cheese. Cover and refrigerate overnight.

Bring the strata to room temperature for 10 to 20 minutes. Preheat the oven to 350°F.

Bake until the custard is set, the casserole is bubbly, and you can't see any liquid when you press the bread lightly, 40 to 45 minutes. Let cool for 10 minutes before serving.

FENNEL-BRAISED PORK ROAST

Serves **8**

4 pounds bone-in, or 3 to 3½ pounds boneless, pork butt or other shoulder roast, rolled and tied

Kosher salt and freshly ground pepper

2 large fennel bulbs, with stalks and fronds

2 large leeks, washed and trimmed

Vegetable or olive oil

3 stalks celery, sliced into 3-inch pieces

1 cup dry white wine

2 sprigs thyme

2 sprigs rosemary

2 bay leaves

½ teaspoon fennel seeds (optional)

3 cups low-sodium chicken or pork broth

Author's Note Bone-in pork roast is harder to find than boneless but is more flavorful. Ask your butcher to roll and tie the roast for you. As with all braises, this is best served the next day, when it is also easier to remove the fat. Let the meat rest in the liquid and refrigerate overnight, then skim off the hardened fat on top.

Editor's Wine Choice Balanced, concentrated red Burgundy: 2011 Louis Jadot Pommard

Fennel and pork are paired often in Italian cooking, such as with the fennel seeds in Italian pork sausage. Pork benefits from sweeter ingredients, and fennel's licorice flavor seems to be the right balance for the rich meat. In this preparation, you braise pork roast with fennel stalks and leek greens, and later add to the pot the white part of the leeks and the fennel bulbs, which are left in large pieces so they don't overcook and can be served with the meat.

Preheat the oven to 325°F. Season the pork roast with salt and pepper and leave at room temperature while you prepare the vegetables. Remove the stalks and fronds from the fennel (reserve and chop some of the fronds to garnish the roast) and chop the stalks into 2-inch chunks. Quarter the bulbs, leaving in the core so they stay intact. Then thickly slice the dark green parts of the leeks to get 1½ cups and cut the white parts into 3-inch lengths. Set aside the fennel bulbs and leek whites.

Heat enough oil to liberally cover the bottom of a Dutch oven over medium to medium-high heat. When the oil is hot, brown the roast until golden all over, 3 to 5 minutes per side. Remove from the pan and pour off all but 1 to 2 tablespoons of fat. Add the leek greens, fennel stalks and fronds, and celery to the pan and cook, stirring to coat, for 2 minutes. Add the wine, deglaze the pan, and simmer for 1 to 2 minutes. Nestle the pork into the vegetables fat side up. Add the thyme, rosemary, bay leaves, and fennel seeds. Pour enough broth to reach halfway up the side of the roast (if you need more liquid, add water), then bring it to a simmer.

Cover and roast for 30 minutes, then remove from the oven. The broth should be at a low simmer; if not, adjust the oven temperature. Flip the roast and continue cooking and flipping every 30 minutes until fork tender, about 3 hours total. After 2 hours, add the leek whites and fennel bulbs.

Remove the pork roast and leek whites and fennel bulb pieces from the Dutch oven, then strain the juices and use a large spoon to scoop off as much of the fat floating on the top as you can. Wipe out the pot, return the juices to the pan, and simmer until thickened, about 10 minutes. To serve, return the meat, fennel bulbs, and leek whites to the Dutch oven and gently rewarm on the stove. Remove the strings from the roast, slice the meat into pieces 1 inch thick, and serve with the juices and vegetables, garnished with the reserved fennel fronds.

SHAVED BROCCOLI STALK SALAD WITH LIME & COTIJA

Serves **2**

Leaves and stalks from 1 bunch broccoli (about 3 stalks), cut into batons (see Author's Prep Tip)

1 tablespoon extra-virgin olive oil

1½ teaspoons fresh lime juice

Kosher salt and freshly ground pepper

¼ cup crumbled Cotija or feta cheese

Author's Prep Tip To make broccoli batons, first remove the stalks at the base of the florets, then trim the tough ends. Cut the stalks into batons by removing the thick, tough outer layer, using four long cuts with a chef's knife.

While waiting for a main course to finish cooking, you can make this simple salad with the remnants of a bunch of broccoli. Or, you can integrate the shaved broccoli, which is sweet, mild, and tender, into other lettuce-based salads, or julienne the strips for cabbage slaws.

Place the broccoli batons flat on a cutting board, then use a sharp vegetable peeler to shave the broccoli into paper-thin strips.

Place the shaved broccoli and leaves in a medium bowl and toss with the olive oil, lime juice, and salt and pepper to taste. Gently fold in the cheese and serve immediately.

GRILLED SNAPPER "TAMALES" WITH CORN-TOMATO SALSA

Total **1 hr**
Serves **4**

SALSA

- 2 ears of corn
- 1 pint cherry tomatoes, quartered
- ½ small red onion, finely chopped
- ¼ cup chopped cilantro
- 1 garlic clove, minced
- 1 serrano chile, minced
- 2 tablespoons fresh lime juice
- ¼ teaspoon ground cumin
- ¼ teaspoon kosher salt

Pepper

FISH

Four 6-ounce skinless red snapper fillets

1½ tablespoons achiote paste (see Note)

1½ tablespoons canola oil, plus more for the grill

- 2 teaspoons fresh lime juice
- ½ teaspoon kosher salt

Lime wedges, for serving

Note Achiote paste is available at Latin markets, specialty food shops and *mexgrocer.com*.

Editor's Wine Choice
Grapefruit-scented, medium-bodied California Sauvignon Blanc: 2013 Geyser Peak

According to Duggan, corn husks are fantastic for wrapping fish on the grill—they keep the fish moist and prevent it from sticking. Just save the husks from shucked corn (you can even freeze them, or substitute dried corn husks often used for tamales) and soak them before wrapping the snapper fillets here.

1. Make the salsa Shuck the corn, leaving on the last thin layer of green husk; reserve all of the husks. Transfer the corn and husks to a large bowl, cover with water and let soak for at least 10 minutes. Drain the corn and husks.

2. Light a grill. Grill the corn over medium heat, turning every 5 minutes, until tender and lightly charred in spots, about 20 minutes. Transfer the corn to a plate and let cool, then remove the husks and silk. Working over a large bowl, cut the kernels from the cobs. Add all of the remaining salsa ingredients except the pepper and mix well; season with pepper. Leave the grill on.

3. Prepare the fish Arrange the fish in a single layer on a baking sheet. In a small bowl, mix the achiote paste with the 1½ tablespoons of canola oil, the lime juice and salt, then rub the paste all over the fish. Lay 2 slightly overlapping corn husks on a work surface and place 1 snapper fillet on top. Lay 2 more overlapping husks on top of the fish to enclose it. Repeat with the remaining corn husks and snapper fillets.

4. Oil the grill grate. Grill the packets over moderately low heat for 4 minutes. Using a large spatula, carefully flip the packets and grill until the fish is just cooked through, 4 to 5 minutes longer. Transfer the "tamales" to plates and unwrap them. Serve the snapper with the salsa and lime wedges.

For more on Tara Duggan
taraduggan.com
Tara Duggan
@taraduggan

Hugh Fearnley-Whittingstall and his family make a dinner out of several vegetarian small plates.

RIVER COTTAGE VEG

200 Inspired Vegetable Recipes

BY **HUGH FEARNLEY-WHITTINGSTALL**

FROM the outset of his new book, Hugh Fearnley-Whittingstall announces his lofty ambitions: He's trying to change the way we eat. The well-known British culinary personality, champion of seasonal and ethically raised food and unabashed carnivore wants us to put vegetables at the center of most of our meals. He has no interest in replacing meat—he just wants to ignore it. His strategy is abundance. Instead of focusing on a single "tyrannical piece of meat," he advocates a small-plates approach to vegetable cooking. Even substantial dishes, like his hearty salad of mushrooms and roasted squash with blue cheese (page 100), can be paired with other sides, such as pistachio *dukka* (page 96)—an Egyptian snack of spices, nuts and seeds—or a luscious sauté of leeks in coconut milk (page 98).

Published by Ten Speed Press, $35

PISTACHIO DUKKA

Makes **about 4 ounces/125 grams**

1 cup/120 grams shelled, unsalted pistachios

1 tablespoon cumin seeds

1 tablespoon coriander seeds

3 tablespoons sesame seeds

A good sprig of mint, leaves only, chopped (optional)

1 teaspoon dried chile flakes

1 teaspoon flaky sea salt

This traditional Egyptian combination of nuts, seeds, and spices is usually served in a small dish, alongside a bowl of olive oil. You dip a piece of bread in the oil, then into the dukka, capturing every last delicious crumb. I sometimes use canola oil for a change. Dukka has other uses, too—try scattering it over grilled vegetables or over a simple salad of lettuce and "soft, hard-boiled" eggs.

If you can only find roasted, salted pistachios, skip the roasting bit and perhaps rub off some of the salt before chopping them. And you can use other nuts—almonds and cashews are particularly good.

Preheat the oven to 400°F/200°C. Scatter the pistachios on a baking sheet and roast in the oven for about 5 minutes, until just starting to turn golden. Cool, then chop them coarsely.

In a dry small frying pan over medium heat, warm the cumin and coriander seeds until they begin to release their aroma. Transfer to a mortar and bash with the pestle until broken up, but not too fine. In the same pan, lightly toast the sesame seeds.

Add the coarsely chopped nuts to the mortar and bash until they are broken up into smallish pieces. Stir in the sesame seeds, mint if using, chile flakes, and salt and transfer to a serving bowl.

The dukka will keep for a couple of weeks at room temperature in a screw-top jar.

This *dukka* doubles as a seasoning to sprinkle on salads.

LEEKS (& GREENS) WITH COCONUT MILK

Serves **4**

4 or 5 medium leeks, trimmed
   of tough ends

About 8 ounces/250 grams
   kale, Swiss chard, or cabbage
   (optional), tough stalks
   removed

2 tablespoons sunflower oil

3 garlic cloves, sliced

1 teaspoon curry powder

1²⁄₃ cups/400 ml coconut milk

2 ounces/60 grams roasted
   peanuts or cashews,
   coarsely chopped or crushed,
   to finish (optional)

I've been cooking this a lot recently—with and without greens. It's great with spicy roasted roots or squash, rice, and maybe some dal on the side. In early summer, when leeks are out of season, I sometimes make it with young green onions instead.

Cut the leeks into ½-inch/1-cm slices on the diagonal. If using greens, shred into ½-inch/1-cm ribbons and set aside.

Heat the sunflower oil in a large frying pan over medium-low heat and sweat the garlic for a couple of minutes, being careful not to let it burn.

Add the leeks and sauté for a few minutes, then add the curry powder and cook, stirring occasionally, for another couple of minutes, until the leeks are becoming tender but still have a bit of bite.

Add the greens, if using, and sweat down for 3 minutes or so, until wilted but still slightly crunchy.

Pour in the coconut milk and heat through, letting it bubble for just a minute. Serve at once, sprinkled with peanuts or cashews if you like.

WARM SALAD OF MUSHROOMS & ROASTED SQUASH

Serves **4**

- 1 small squash, such as butternut, acorn, or red kuri, or ½ larger one (about 2 pounds/1 kg)
- 12 sage leaves, bruised
- 4 garlic cloves, thickly sliced
- 7 tablespoons/100 ml canola or olive oil
- Sea salt and freshly ground black pepper
- About 1 tablespoon butter
- 10 ounces/300 grams open-cap mushrooms, thickly sliced
- A small bunch of arugula
- 5 ounces/150 grams blue cheese, crumbled

FOR THE DRESSING

- 3 tablespoons canola or olive oil
- 1 tablespoon balsamic vinegar (ideally apple balsamic)
- Sea salt and freshly ground black pepper

Editor's Wine Choice Ripe, minerally Chenin Blanc: 2012 François Chidaine Les Argiles Vouvray

This substantial salad is something of a River Cottage classic, and a great way to bring together two of autumn's finest ingredients: mushrooms and squash. Blue cheese is quite delicious here, but you could use other cheeses—shavings of Parmesan, a hard goat cheese such as Ticklemore, or a firm sheep's milk cheese such as Berkswell would also work well.

Preheat the oven to 375°F/190°C. Peel, halve, and seed the squash. Cut into 1-inch/2.5-cm chunks and put into a roasting pan with the sage leaves, garlic, 6 tablespoons of the oil, and a generous seasoning of salt and pepper. Roast for about 40 minutes, stirring once, or until the squash is soft and colored at the edges.

Put the remaining 1 tablespoon of oil in a frying pan with the butter and place over medium heat. Throw in the mushrooms along with a little salt and pepper and fry for 4 to 5 minutes, or until the mushrooms are cooked through and any liquid they release has evaporated.

For the dressing, in a small bowl, whisk together the oil and balsamic vinegar and season with some salt and pepper.

In a large bowl, combine the still-warm (but not hot) cooked squash and mushrooms with the arugula and cheese. Add enough dressing to lightly coat the ingredients (you may not need it all), toss together, and serve.

For more on Hugh Fearnley-Whittingstall
rivercottage.net
 River Cottage
 @rivercottage

"The brilliance of rustic Italian food is its simplicity," says Francine Stephens, here with her husband, Andrew Feinberg.

FRANNY'S

Simple Seasonal Italian

BY **ANDREW FEINBERG, FRANCINE STEPHENS**
& **MELISSA CLARK**

TRY the spaghetti with artichokes (page 106) and you'll see what's so impressive about this Italian cookbook: Andrew Feinberg and Francine Stephens's recipe requires only a few steps for spectacular results. The owners of Brooklyn's Franny's excel at the ingredient-first food philosophy they helped pioneer when they opened their restaurant in 2004 and began showcasing the freshest farmers' market ingredients. "Simple is better," they write. "Once you have the best ingredients you can find, you won't need to do much to them." True to the spirit of *cucina povera* (poverty cuisine), Feinberg and Stephens really commit themselves to the minimalist recipes that have made Franny's one of New York City's best-loved restaurants.

Published by Artisan, $35

SUGAR SNAP PEAS WITH RICOTTA, MINT & LEMON

Serves **4**

½ cup whole-milk ricotta

¼ cup extra-virgin olive oil, plus more for drizzling

Kosher salt

¼ teaspoon freshly cracked black pepper, plus more to taste

2 cups sugar snap peas (½ pound)

2 tablespoons thinly sliced scallions

2 tablespoons coarsely chopped flat-leaf parsley

3 tablespoons coarsely chopped mint

2 tablespoons fresh lemon juice

Flaky sea salt, such as Maldon

Editor's Wine Choice Floral, mandarin orange–scented Sicilian white: 2012 Occhipinti SP68 Bianco

This springtime dish is crisp and sweet from the sugar snap peas, creamy from a layer of seasoned ricotta, and bright and fresh from a dressing of fragrant mint leaves, scallions, and parsley. It's almost like a very elegant crudité, and who doesn't love dipping crunchy vegetables into creamy dip? My kids certainly do, and this recipe is a great way to turn little ones on to the joys of green things. The sugar snap peas are intrinsically sweet, and they're ideal finger-food-size for little hands.

Line a fine-mesh sieve with cheesecloth or a clean dish towel, set over a bowl, and add the ricotta. Refrigerate overnight; the ricotta will lose much of its water content and thicken.

In a small bowl, whisk the drained ricotta with 2 tablespoons of the olive oil until smooth. Whisk in salt and pepper to taste. Continue to whisk until the ricotta is fluffy and creamy. Set aside.

Bring a large pot of salted water to a boil. Fill a large bowl with ice water and salt it generously. Blanch the peas in the boiling water for 30 to 40 seconds, until bright green. Drain, immediately transfer to the ice water, and let stand until thoroughly chilled. Drain the peas and spread them out on a clean dish towel to dry.

In a large bowl, toss the peas with the scallions, parsley, mint, the ¼ teaspoon pepper, and the lemon juice. Stir in the remaining 2 tablespoons olive oil.

Smear 2 tablespoons of the ricotta in the center of each of four plates. Mound ½ cup of the peas on each plate. Finish with a drizzle of olive oil and a sprinkle of sea salt.

ANDREW'S NOTE To get perfectly seasoned snap peas (and other dense vegetables, for that matter), blanch them in boiling salted water, drain them, and then cool them in salted ice water. Don't overcook sugar snap peas; they should literally be in and out of a pot of boiling water—just 30 to 40 seconds—then plunged directly into an ice bath. Any longer, and you risk losing their crisp texture.

SPAGHETTI WITH ARTICHOKES

Serves **4**

- 8 **small or 4 large artichokes, trimmed (see Tip below)**
- ¾ **cup extra-virgin olive oil, plus more for drizzling**
- 8 **garlic cloves, smashed and peeled**
- 2 **teaspoons kosher salt**
- ½ **teaspoon chili flakes**
- ½ **cup water**
- 1 **pound spaghetti**
- ½ **cup chopped flat-leaf parsley**
- 3 **tablespoons finely grated Parmigiano-Reggiano**
- 1 **tablespoon unsalted butter**
- ¼ **teaspoon freshly cracked black pepper**
- 4 **teaspoons finely grated Pecorino Romano, plus more if desired**

Editor's Wine Choice Ripe, fruit-forward Italian white: 2012 Sergio Mottura Poggio della Costa Grechetto

The flavors in this recipe are very Roman: a combination of artichokes and Pecorino Romano, along with chili, garlic, and parsley, is something you'd see in a trattoria in the Eternal City. We like the addition of the softer Parmigiano-Reggiano, which imparts a milky creaminess to balance out the Pecorino's piquant saltiness.

Halve the artichokes lengthwise, then slice lengthwise into ¼-inch-thick slices. In a very large skillet (or a Dutch oven; see Tip on page 112), warm the olive oil over medium-high heat. Add the artichokes, garlic, and salt and cook until the artichokes are nicely browned and a little soft and the garlic is golden around the edges, 6 to 7 minutes. Add the chili flakes and cook for 1 minute. Add the water (just enough to not quite cover the artichokes) and let simmer until the artichokes are very soft, about 2 minutes. There should still be some liquid remaining in the pan. Remove from the heat.

Meanwhile in a large pot of well-salted boiling water, cook the pasta according to package instructions until 2 minutes shy of al dente; drain. Toss the spaghetti into the skillet with the artichokes, parsley, Parmigiano-Reggiano, butter, and pepper, and cook until the pasta is just al dente, 1 to 2 minutes. Add 2 tablespoons water if the sauce seems dry.

Divide the pasta among four individual serving plates or bowls; finish each with a drizzle of olive oil and a teaspoon or more of Pecorino Romano.

TIP To prepare the artichokes: Fill a large bowl with cold water and add the juice of two lemons. As you trim the artichokes, dip them occasionally into the lemon water to prevent browning. Pull off and discard the outer leaves of each artichoke until you reach the pale green leaves at the center. Using a paring knife, trim away the dark green skin from the base. Slice off the very tip of the stem: you will see a pale green core in the stem, surrounded by a layer of darker green; use a paring knife to trim away as much of the dark green layer as possible; the white part of the stem is as tasty as the heart. Slice off the top third of the artichoke at the place where the dark green tops fade to pale green. Using a teaspoon (a serrated grapefruit spoon is perfect for this task), scoop out the hairy choke in the center of the artichoke, pulling out any pointed purple leaves with your fingers as well. The center of the artichoke should be completely clean. Drop the artichoke into the lemon water.

CHICKPEA & KALE SOUP

Serves **8 to 10**

2 cups dried chickpeas

1 carrot, peeled and cut into large chunks

1 celery stalk, cut into large chunks

1 onion, halved

11 garlic cloves

5 strips lemon peel

1 rosemary sprig

1 tablespoon kosher salt, or more to taste

3½ quarts water

1½ cups plus 2 tablespoons extra-virgin olive oil, plus more for drizzling

¼ teaspoon chili flakes

2 bunches Tuscan kale

Freshly cracked black pepper

Lemon wedges

Finely grated Parmigiano-Reggiano

As far as we know, there's no classic Italian soup made with chickpeas and kale. This was born out of our love for the combination of Tuscan kale and chickpeas, which work beautifully together. Andrew came up with the recipe one day when he noticed that the broth left from cooking chickpeas was so delicious it was practically begging to be made into soup. So he did just that, adding fresh kale to the pot and letting it simmer until soft and silky. With its bright, deeply green color, this soup is as beautiful as it is delicious.

Place the chickpeas in a large bowl and cover with plenty of water. Let soak for 8 hours or overnight; drain.

Wrap the carrot, celery, onion, 3 garlic cloves, the lemon peel, and rosemary in a large square of cheesecloth and secure with kitchen twine or a tight knot.

In a large pot, combine the sachet of vegetables, the chickpeas, salt, water, and 1 cup of the olive oil. Bring to a boil over high heat, then reduce the heat to medium-low and simmer until the chickpeas are tender, about 1 hour.

Meanwhile, finely chop the remaining 8 garlic cloves. In a small skillet, heat 3 tablespoons olive oil over medium heat. Add the garlic and chili flakes and cook until the garlic is fragrant but not golden, about 1 minute. Remove from the heat.

Remove the center ribs from the kale and coarsely chop the leaves (you should have about 16 cups). In a large skillet, heat the remaining 7 tablespoons olive oil over medium-high heat. Add the kale in batches and cook, tossing occasionally, until tender, about 3 minutes. Remove from the heat.

When the chickpeas are cooked, combine the kale, garlic oil, 2 cups of the chickpeas, and 1 cup of the cooking liquid in a food processor and puree until smooth. Return the puree to the pot and cook over medium-high heat until hot. Season with salt and pepper to taste.

Ladle the soup into bowls. Finish with a squeeze of lemon, some grated Parmigiano-Reggiano, and a drizzle of olive oil.

FUSILLI WITH PORK SAUSAGE RAGU

Serves **4 to 6**

- 2 tablespoons unsalted butter
- 2 tablespoons extra-virgin olive oil
- 2½ pounds coarsely ground pork
- ⅔ cup ¼-inch-diced pancetta (3½ ounces)
- ½ teaspoon chili flakes
- 3 large garlic cloves, minced
- 1 medium onion, minced
- ⅔ cup finely diced carrots
- ⅔ cup finely diced celery
- ⅔ cup chopped flat-leaf parsley
- 3½ tablespoons tomato paste
- ⅔ cup dry red wine
- One 14-ounce can Italian cherry tomatoes, drained and smashed, or canned diced tomatoes
- 2 cups water
- 2 teaspoons kosher salt, plus more to taste
- Freshly cracked black pepper
- 1 pound fusilli
- Finely grated Parmigiano-Reggiano and fresh ricotta for finishing

Editor's Wine Choice
Smooth, dark-fruited Italian red: 2011 Foradori Teroldego

This is one of the most popular dishes at Franny's. Instead of taking big cuts of meat and braising them until they fall apart, we grind the meat and aggressively season it, thereby making a kind of ad hoc sausage meat. The flavor notes here are very much those of Southern Italy, with a touch of rich tomato paste and a dash of chili. Pancetta, with its porky richness, adds another dimension. Fusilli, offering up all those nooks and crannies in which the sausage can hide, makes the perfect companion to this ragu.

In a heavy stockpot or a Dutch oven, melt the butter with the olive oil over medium-high heat. Add the ground pork (cook in batches if necessary) and cook just until golden; be careful not to overbrown. Using a slotted spoon, remove the meat from the pot and set aside.

Add the pancetta to the pot and cook gently over medium heat until the fat is rendered and the meat begins to crisp. Stir in the chili flakes and garlic and cook until fragrant, about 1 minute. Add the onion, carrots, celery, and parsley and cook until the onion is translucent, 10 to 15 minutes. Stir in the tomato paste and cook for 2 minutes, then add the red wine and bring to a simmer.

Add the pork to the pot, along with the tomatoes, water, and salt. Bring the mixture to a simmer, cover the pot with a tight-fitting lid, and simmer for 40 minutes.

Remove the lid and continue to simmer until the ragu has thickened nicely, 15 to 20 minutes longer. Season to taste with salt and pepper.

Let the ragu cool to room temperature, then refrigerate until thoroughly chilled.

Remove and discard about two-thirds of the fat that has settled on the surface of the ragu, leaving the remaining third to be incorporated back into the sauce.

continued on page 112

Stirring in
the ricotta
at the end
makes the
sauce creamy.

FUSILLI WITH PORK SAUSAGE RAGU *continued*

In a large pot of well-salted boiling water, cook the pasta according to the package instructions until 2 minutes shy of al dente; drain.

While the pasta is cooking, in a very large skillet (or a Dutch oven; see Tip), warm the ragu over medium heat.

Toss the fusilli into the skillet with the ragu and cook until al dente, 1 to 2 minutes. If the sauce seems dry, add a few tablespoons of water.

Divide the pasta among four individual serving plates or bowls. Finish each with a sprinkle of Parmigiano-Reggiano and a dollop of ricotta.

TIP Dutch ovens have higher sides than skillets, making it harder to evaporate liquid. They also retain heat beautifully—which is good for braises but not for pasta, as too much residual heat in the pot can wilt the noodles. If using a Dutch oven, make sure the sauce is cooked down until it's thick before you add the pasta, then go light when adding water to the pan. As soon as the pasta is ready, serve it or transfer it to a warmed serving platter. You don't want it to sit in the hot pot and continue to cook.

TURNIP-APPLE SOUP

Total **1 hr**
Serves **4**

2 tablespoons extra-virgin olive oil

1½ pounds turnips (preferably Gilfeather or hakurei), peeled and sliced ¼ inch thick

Kosher salt

2 tablespoons unsalted butter

1 small onion, finely chopped

1 celery stalk, finely chopped

1 shallot, finely chopped

3 garlic cloves, finely chopped

1 Granny Smith apple, peeled and chopped into ½-inch pieces

2 tablespoons heavy cream

When Franny's chef John Adler tasted sweet, just-picked turnips and apples together at the farmers' market, he was inspired to create this silky soup. "I realized that these two ingredients belong together," he says. Adler prefers to use Gilfeather or hakurei turnips (also called Tokyo turnips), which are milder and sweeter than the supermarket variety.

1. In a large saucepan, heat 1 tablespoon of the oil. Add half of the turnips, season with salt and cook over moderate heat, stirring occasionally, until golden, about 5 minutes. Transfer the turnips to a plate and repeat with the remaining 1 tablespoon of oil and the rest of the turnips.

2. In the same saucepan, combine the butter, onion, celery, shallot, garlic, apple and turnips. Season with salt and cook, stirring occasionally, until the vegetables are softened, 7 to 8 minutes. Stir in 4 cups of water and bring to a boil. Cover and cook over low heat until the turnips are very tender, about 25 minutes.

3. Transfer the mixture to a blender, add the cream and puree until smooth. Season the soup with salt and serve warm.

MAKE AHEAD The soup can be refrigerated for up to 2 days.

For more on Franny's
frannysbrooklyn.com
 Franny's
🐦 @frannysbk

BLUEBERRY–VANILLA
CREAM HAND PIES,
P.116

SWEET

BY **VALERIE GORDON**

OVER the past ten years, Valerie Gordon has gone from selling six kinds of chocolates out of her dining room to making elaborate cakes, pies and pastries for her Los Angeles boutique and retailers nationwide. Her debut cookbook includes the recipe for her original dining room–created sweets (featuring a sprinkle of fleur de sel, to which she attributes their overnight superstardom), as well as detailed and highly specific descriptions of basic dessert skills, like how to make the dough for her sweet and tart blueberry–vanilla cream hand pies (pictured at left). And if her chocolates hadn't made her famous, her perfectly crusty-chewy brownies (page 122) surely would have.

Published by Artisan, $35

BLUEBERRY–VANILLA CREAM HAND PIES

Makes **15 hand pies**

Pie Dough (recipe follows)

1 cup (8 ounces) Vanilla Cream (recipe follows)

3 cups (12 ounces) blueberries, rinsed and dried

1 egg, beaten

Sugar for dusting

Bright, tart berry flavors are deliciously enhanced when juxtaposed with sweet vanilla-specked cream. The flavors and textures of a pie à la mode are paired inside these delicious hand pies. Serve at room temperature, or reheat for 5 minutes in a 300°F oven.

Position the racks in the upper and lower thirds of the oven and heat the oven to 350°F. Line two 13-by-18-by-1-inch baking sheets with parchment or silicone liners.

Remove the dough from the refrigerator and place one disk on a floured cool surface. Using a rolling pin, roll the dough out approximately ⅛ inch thick: Start from the center of the dough and roll outward, rotating the dough 2 to 3 inches after each roll. After every four to five rolls, run a large offset spatula under the dough to release it from the work surface. Add a little flour to the surface, rolling pin, and/or dough if the dough sticks or becomes difficult to roll.

Using a 4-inch ring mold, cut out rounds and place on one of the lined baking sheets; reserve the scraps. Refrigerate until ready to use. Repeat the rolling process with the second disk of dough. If you have fewer than 15 rounds, pile the dough scraps together, wrap in plastic, and chill until firm, then roll out and cut out more rounds.

Remove the first sheet of dough from the refrigerator. Spoon 1 tablespoon vanilla cream, leaving a border, and then 4 to 6 blueberries onto one half of one round. Using a pastry brush, brush the beaten egg around the edges of the dough. Lift the empty side of the round over the filling and slowly drape the dough over the fruit so the two edges meet. (If you force the dough, it may crack or tear; gently cajoling the dough will help it soften and yield.) Gently press the edges of the dough together and then, using a fork, crimp the edges to seal them. Repeat with the remaining rounds, then repeat with the second sheet of rounds. Refrigerate the pies until the crusts are cold and firm to the touch, about 15 minutes. (Reserve the remaining beaten egg.)

Brush the top and edge of each pie with beaten egg and dust with a little sugar. Slash the top of each pie once or twice with a paring knife to create a steam vent.

Bake for 20 minutes. Rotate the pans and bake for an additional 15 minutes, or until the pies are golden brown and oozing juices. Cool completely on the baking sheets, then remove with an offset spatula.

STORING The pies can be stored, covered, at room temperature for up to 2 days.

Pie Dough

Given the choice between a piecrust made with butter and one made with shortening, I always choose butter. If you keep your dough cold at every step of the way, you can achieve the same flakiness that people attribute to shortening with the incomparable flavor of butter.

Makes enough for **one 9-inch double-crust pie, two 9-inch single-crust pies, or fifteen 4-inch hand pies**

2½ cups (12.5 ounces) all-purpose flour

2 teaspoons sugar

1 teaspoon salt

2½ sticks (10 ounces) unsalted butter, cubed and chilled

¼ to ⅓ cup (2 to 2.5 ounces) cold water

To make the dough in a food processor Put the flour, sugar, and salt in the processor bowl and pulse once or twice to combine. Drop the pieces of butter through the feed tube, continuing to pulse until the mixture resembles coarse crumbs. Slowly add ¼ cup water as you continue pulsing a few more times, then add more water if necessary; stop when the dough just starts to come together.

To make the dough by hand Put the flour, sugar, and salt into a medium bowl and mix together with a fork or small whisk. Cut the butter into the dough using a pastry cutter or a large fork until the mixture resembles coarse crumbs. Drizzle ¼ cup water directly over the dough, mixing with the pastry cutter or fork, then add more water if necessary, mixing until the dough just comes together.

Remove the dough from the processor or bowl and form into 2 equal disks. Wrap each disk in plastic wrap and refrigerate for at least 2 hours, or up to 3 days. The dough can be frozen for up to 2 months; thaw in the refrigerator.

continued on page 118

BLUEBERRY–VANILLA CREAM HAND PIES *continued*

Makes **about 1½ cups**

¾ cup (6 ounces) whole milk

¼ cup (1.75 ounces) granulated sugar

1 tablespoon light brown sugar

½ vanilla bean, split, seeds scraped out, seeds and bean reserved, or 1 teaspoon vanilla bean paste (see Resource)

¼ cup (2 ounces) heavy cream

2 large egg yolks

2 tablespoons cornstarch

2 tablespoons (1 ounce) unsalted butter, cut into small chunks

Vanilla Cream

Combine the milk, granulated sugar, brown sugar, and vanilla seeds and bean in a medium saucepan and bring just to a simmer over medium-low heat, stirring constantly. Turn off the heat and remove the vanilla bean.

Whisk together the heavy cream, egg yolks, and cornstarch in a medium bowl. Continue whisking as you slowly stream in the hot milk mixture. (Put a dish towel underneath the bowl so it stays still while you're whisking.) Pour the vanilla cream back into the pan and cook over medium-low heat, whisking constantly, until the cream thickens. Remove from the heat and stir in the butter until melted.

Pour the cream through a fine-mesh sieve into a medium bowl. Cover the surface of the cream with plastic wrap so it doesn't form a skin, and refrigerate until cold, about 2 hours.

The cream can be stored in an airtight container, refrigerated, for up to 1 week.

RESOURCE Surfas, *www.culinarydistrict.com*. Almond flours, almond paste, chocolates in a wide range of percentages, candied (crystallized) ginger, edible gold leaf, vanilla beans, vanilla bean paste, and a large assortment of other specialty baking and confection ingredients, as well as equipment.

RASPBERRY–VANILLA BEAN CRUMBLE MUFFINS

Makes **12 muffins**

FOR THE CRUMBLE

- ¾ cup (3.75 ounces) all-purpose flour
- 1 cup (6 ounces) light brown sugar
- 1 teaspoon ground cinnamon
- ½ teaspoon kosher salt
- 5 tablespoons (2.5 ounces) unsalted butter, cubed and chilled

FOR THE MUFFINS

- 2 cups (10 ounces) all-purpose flour
- 2 teaspoons baking powder
- ½ teaspoon kosher salt
- 5 tablespoons (2.5 ounces) unsalted butter, softened
- 1 cup (7 ounces) granulated sugar
- 1 large egg
- ½ cup (4 ounces) heavy cream
- 2 teaspoons vanilla bean paste (see Resource on previous page)
- 2 cups (8 ounces) raspberries, rinsed and dried

Is this a muffin or a cake? The line between breakfast pastry and dessert is sometimes hazy at best, and here we have an excellent example of that conundrum.

Position a rack in the center of the oven and heat the oven to 350°F. Line a muffin tin with muffin liners.

To make the crumble Combine the flour, brown sugar, cinnamon, and salt in a food processor, and pulse to blend. With the processor running, add the butter, pulsing until the mixture looks like sand, about 2 minutes. Set aside.

To make the muffins Sift together the flour, baking powder, and salt into a medium bowl.

In the bowl of a stand mixer fitted with the paddle attachment (or in a large bowl, using a handheld mixer), cream the butter and sugar on medium speed until light and fluffy, about 3 minutes.

Mix the egg, heavy cream, and vanilla paste together in a small bowl with a fork or small whisk. Add to the creamed butter and mix until fully combined, about 2 minutes; the batter will appear a little lumpy. Add the dry ingredients in two batches, mixing well after each addition. Scrape down the sides and bottom of the bowl and the paddle attachment. Use a rubber spatula to fold in the raspberries to avoid crushing them.

Using an ice cream scoop or a large spoon, scoop about ⅓ cup batter into each muffin cup. Pick up the muffin tin and knock it firmly against the work surface a couple of times to level the batter and release any air pockets. Cover the top of each muffin with 1 tablespoon of the crumble.

Bake for 13 minutes, then rotate the muffin tin and bake for an additional 14 minutes, or until a toothpick inserted in the center of a muffin comes out clean. Cool the muffins in the pan on a cooling rack for 15 to 20 minutes before removing them.

STORING The muffins can be stored for up to 2 days in an airtight container or frozen for up to 2 months in Ziploc freezer bags.

CHOCOLATE GRANOLA

Makes **about 12 cups**

4 cups (13 ounces) rolled oats

1½ cups (5.25 ounces) sliced raw almonds

1 cup (3.5 ounces) raw hazelnuts, halved

¼ cup (1 ounce) cocoa nibs (see Resource below)

⅓ cup (1.3 ounces) unsweetened cocoa powder

¾ cup (4.5 ounces) light brown sugar

¼ cup (2.75 ounces) honey

⅓ cup (2.36 ounces) canola oil

2 teaspoons vanilla bean paste (see Resource on page 118)

8.25 ounces 61 percent bittersweet chocolate, finely chopped

1½ teaspoons fleur de sel

Granola has taken on a new identity of late; I see it frequently on salads or cheese platters. This one is for dessert. It includes all the defining ingredients of granola, but then it goes in a different direction. With the chocolate, it is best served on ice cream or pudding or another sweet.

Heat the oven to 250°F. Line two 13-by-18-by-1-inch baking sheets with parchment paper or silicone liners.

In a large bowl, mix the oats, almonds, hazelnuts, and cocoa nibs.

Mix the cocoa powder, sugar, honey, oil, and vanilla paste in a small bowl, stirring well. Pour over the dry ingredients and stir with a rubber spatula until the dry ingredients are evenly moistened.

Spread the granola on one of the prepared baking sheets. Bake for about 1 hour, stirring every 15 minutes, until the nuts are slightly golden.

Quickly pour the hot granola onto the second baking sheet and spread it evenly. Sprinkle the chopped chocolate evenly over the granola and wait for 1 to 2 minutes; the chocolate will melt. Spread the chocolate evenly with an offset spatula, then sprinkle the fleur de sel over the chocolate and move the pan to a cool area. Allow the granola to cool for 15 to 20 minutes. If the chocolate has not set, put the pan in the refrigerator until it is firm to touch, 5 to 10 minutes, then bring back to room temperature. Break up the granola.

STORING The granola can be stored in an airtight container for up to 3 weeks.

RESOURCE Valrhona, *www.valrhona-chocolate.com*. Exceptional chocolates for baking and all chocolate work, including cocoa nibs.

Cocoa nibs, the secret ingredient, add a nicely bitter crunch.

BROWNIES

Makes **9 large brownies**
or **18 small brownies**

12 tablespoons (1½ sticks/
    6 ounces) unsalted butter

 3 ounces 99 percent unsweetened
    chocolate, chopped

 1 cup (7 ounces) granulated sugar

 ½ cup (3 ounces) light brown
    sugar

 3 large eggs

 ¾ cup (3.75 ounces) all-purpose
    flour

 1 teaspoon vanilla bean paste
    (see Resource on page 118)

 1 teaspoon kosher salt

This recipe delivers all the best parts of a brownie: crispy edges, a chewy center, and a slight crunch to the crust. In order to maximize the best brownie attributes, the batter is spread thin for a better crust, and brown sugar is blended with white to increase the chewiness factor.

Heat the oven to 350°F. Butter the bottom and sides of a 9-by-9-by-2-inch square baking pan and line the bottom with parchment paper or aluminum foil.

Melt the butter and chocolate in a double boiler or a medium heatproof bowl set over a pot of boiling water, stirring occasionally with a small whisk until smooth. Remove from the heat and let cool for 2 to 3 minutes. If you used a double boiler, transfer the chocolate to a medium bowl.

Stir both sugars into the chocolate mixture until fully combined. Using a rubber spatula or a wooden spoon, mix in the eggs one at a time. Add the flour, vanilla paste, and salt, and stir until thoroughly combined.

Spread the batter into the prepared baking pan. Bake for 25 to 30 minutes, until a crust forms and the center appears dry. Check the brownies with a toothpick—small crumbs should adhere (do not bake until a toothpick inserted in the center comes out totally clean). Let the brownies cool in the pan for at least 10 minutes on a cooling rack before cutting with a sharp knife.

STORING Once cooled, the brownies can be stored in an airtight container for up to 5 days; or leave the brownies, uncut, in the pan, wrap in a double layer of plastic wrap, and freeze for up to 2 months.

BLOOD ORANGE PANNA COTTA PARFAITS

Active **25 min**; Total **50 min plus 5 hr chilling**
Makes **8 parfaits**

PANNA COTTA

- 1¼ cups fresh blood orange juice, strained
- 1 cup sugar
- 2 teaspoons unflavored powdered gelatin
- 2 tablespoons cold water
- 3½ cups heavy cream

GELÉE

- 1 teaspoon unflavored powdered gelatin
- 1 tablespoon cold water
- 1¼ cups fresh blood orange juice, strained
- ¼ cup plus 2 tablespoons sugar

This stunning dessert—creamy, luscious, bright and tart all at once—features blood orange in both the panna cotta and the thin layer of gelée on top.

1. Make the panna cotta In a medium saucepan, combine the blood orange juice with 2 tablespoons of the sugar and cook over moderately high heat, stirring occasionally with a wooden spoon, until the juice is reduced to ⅔ cup, about 12 minutes. Meanwhile, in a small bowl, sprinkle the gelatin over the cold water and let stand until softened, about 10 minutes.

2. Add the softened gelatin to the reduced juice along with the cream and the remaining ¾ cup plus 2 tablespoons of sugar. Cook over moderately low heat, stirring occasionally, until the gelatin has melted, about 5 minutes; do not let the mixture boil. Ladle the panna cotta mixture into 8 small glasses (about ⅔ cup in each) and refrigerate until firm and set, at least 3 hours.

3. Make the gelée In a small bowl, sprinkle the gelatin over the cold water and let stand until softened, about 5 minutes. In a medium saucepan, combine the blood orange juice with the sugar and softened gelatin and cook over moderately low heat, stirring occasionally, until the gelatin has melted, about 3 minutes; do not let the mixture boil. Let cool for 10 minutes.

4. Carefully spoon the gelée over the panna cotta layer (about 3 tablespoons in each glass). Cover and refrigerate the parfaits until the gelée is set, about 2 hours.

MAKE AHEAD The parfaits can be refrigerated for up to 2 days.

For more on Valerie Gordon
valerieconfections.com
[f] Valerie Confections
[t] @ValerieConfctns

Will Guidara (left) with Daniel Humm
on the Brooklyn Bridge; the duo
often walk across to brainstorm.

I LOVE NEW YORK

Ingredients & Recipes

BY **DANIEL HUMM** & **WILL GUIDARA**

THE new book from Daniel Humm and Will Guidara–chef and general manager, respectively, of the revered Eleven Madison Park in Manhattan–is a tribute to the city they love and its food producers and surrounding farms. Some of the surprisingly straightforward recipes are Humm's innovations, like the soothing mashed zucchini with mint (page 128) and perfectly cooked rack of lamb with cucumber yogurt (page 130). Other recipes, like Delmonico steak (page 126)–a boneless rib eye bathed in herb butter–pay homage to New York City's culinary icons. The recipes add up to a world-class chef's guided tour of his favorite food and purveyors in and around the city.

Published by Ten Speed Press, $50

DELMONICO STEAK

Serves **4**

HERB BUTTER

- 1 **pound butter, at room temperature**
- 1 **tablespoon chopped chervil**
- 1 **tablespoon chopped chives**
- 1 **tablespoon chopped parsley**
- 1 **tablespoon chopped tarragon**

Zest of 1 lemon

1½ tablespoons sea salt

STEAK

- 2 **tablespoons canola oil**

Four ¾-pound boneless rib-eye steaks, about 1 inch thick

Salt

Ground black pepper

- 1 **tablespoon butter**
- 5 **sprigs thyme**
- 1 **clove garlic**

Editor's Wine Choice Cedar- and cassis-scented Napa Valley Cabernet Sauvignon: 2009 Heitz Cellar

The legendary Delmonico's, which opened in the financial district in 1837, revolutionized restaurants. It was the first in the U.S. to go by the French term *restaurant*, the first to allow women to dine without a male escort, the first to have printed menus, the first to have a wine list, the first to use tablecloths, and the first to have diners sit at private tables. It was there that American classics like lobster Newburg, eggs Benedict, and baked Alaska came into existence. Of all of the Delmonico's dishes, though, the most legendary is perhaps Delmonico steak, a dish whose exact preparation and exact cut of meat remain a mystery. In the years after the original Delmonico's closed its doors, a series of imitators opened restaurants called "Delmonico's" around the city, and in the process, the precise cut originally used for this fabled dish was lost along the way. The true identity of the Delmonico steak is thus one of the food world's enduring enigmas.

Herb butter Place all of the ingredients in a mixing bowl and combine with a spatula. Place on a sheet of plastic wrap and roll into a cylinder. Alternatively, use a piping bag and star tip to create small rosettes. Refrigerate until firm.

Steak Heat the oil in a 10-inch cast-iron skillet over high heat until it just begins to smoke. Season the steaks with salt and pepper and sear in the skillet until golden, 2 to 3 minutes. Flip the steaks and sear for an additional 2 to 3 minutes. Add the butter, thyme, and garlic. Lower the heat to medium-low and baste the steaks for 1 minute with the foamy brown butter. Flip and repeat. Repeat this process for 7 to 8 minutes, flipping the steaks every minute and basting until the internal temperature reaches 130° to 135°F. Allow the steaks to rest for 10 minutes before serving with herb butter.

NOTE Any leftover herb butter can be tightly wrapped and frozen for up to 1 month. It is great with steak and roasted vegetables or potatoes.

MASHED ZUCCHINI WITH MINT

Serves **4**

SAUTÉED ZUCCHINI

8 large zucchini

¼ cup olive oil

2 cloves garlic, crushed but kept whole

TO FINISH

20 mint leaves

10 squash blossoms

Salt

Sautéed zucchini Slice the top and bottom ends off of the zucchini. Cut down the length of the zucchini so the seeds remain separate from the skin and flesh. Rotate the zucchini, and do the same on the remaining three sides. You will be left with four strips of flesh and skin and a rectangle of just seeds; discard the seeds.

Heat a large straight-sided pan over medium-high heat and add the olive oil. Add the garlic and cook until golden, 2 to 3 minutes. Add the zucchini to the pan, raise the heat to high, and cook, stirring frequently to prevent the zucchini from taking on any color. Cover with a parchment paper lid. Turn down the heat to medium-low and continue cooking until the zucchini is tender, 7 to 8 minutes.

To finish Stack 5 mint leaves at a time on top of one another and slice into ribbons. Trim off and discard the bottoms of the squash blossoms and slice the blossoms into ribbons as you did the mint. Mash the sautéed zucchini in a serving bowl with a fork. Fold in the mint and squash blossoms and season with salt to taste.

LAMB RACK WITH CUCUMBER YOGURT

Serves **4**

CUCUMBER YOGURT

1½ cups plain Greek-style yogurt

2 cucumbers

Salt

2 teaspoons lemon juice

1 tablespoon olive oil

½ clove garlic

1½ tablespoons chopped dill

ROASTED LAMB RACK

1 tablespoon canola oil

1 lamb rack (about 2¼ pounds), frenched and tied

Salt

2 tablespoons butter

5 sprigs thyme

1 clove garlic, crushed but kept whole

Editor's Wine Choice
Peppery Languedoc red: 2011
Clos Fantine Faugères

Cucumber yogurt Line a colander with a quadruple layer of cheesecloth and pour the yogurt into the cheesecloth. Suspend over a large bowl and refrigerate for 48 hours, allowing the moisture to drain from the yogurt.

Peel and grate the cucumbers on a box grater. Season with 1 teaspoon of salt and hang in a quadruple layer of cheesecloth to drain excess moisture, about 1 hour. Measure 1 cup of the drained yogurt and reserve the rest for another use. Combine the cup of yogurt and the drained cucumbers in a medium bowl. Stir in the lemon juice and olive oil. Grate the garlic on a Microplane grater into the mixture and fold in the chopped dill. Mix well and season with salt to taste.

Roasted lamb rack Preheat the oven to 300°F. Heat the oil in a large cast-iron skillet over high heat. Season the lamb rack generously with salt. Place the rack in the skillet fat side down and sear over high heat until browned, 2½ to 3 minutes. Turn and sear the bottom for 1 minute. Turn the rack back onto the fat side and add the butter, thyme, and garlic. Baste the rack with the butter for 2½ to 3 minutes. Transfer the lamb rack fat side up to a wire rack set in a rimmed baking sheet and roast in the oven for 10 minutes. Turn the lamb rack over, baste with butter, and return to the oven for another 10 minutes. Remove the lamb rack from the oven, turn it back over, and baste once more. Roast in the oven for another 10 to 15 minutes, until the internal temperature reaches 130° to 135°F. Let the lamb rack rest for 10 to 15 minutes before slicing. Serve with the cucumber yogurt and heirloom tomatoes.

Butter-basting
the lamb
keeps it moist
as it cooks.

RADICCHIO WITH GRANNY SMITH APPLES & MOZZARELLA

Total **30 min**
Serves **4**

MARINATED APPLES

- 2 **tablespoons fresh lemon juice**
- 3 **tablespoons extra-virgin olive oil**
- 2 **tablespoons lemon oil**

Kosher salt

- 1 **Granny Smith apple, cored and cut into ⅛-inch-thick wedges**

APPLE VINAIGRETTE

- 3 **tablespoons apple cider vinegar**
- 3 **tablespoons extra-virgin olive oil**
- 3 **tablespoons grapeseed oil**
- 1 **teaspoon sugar**
- ½ **teaspoon kosher salt**

SALAD

Six 1-inch mozzarella balls (3 ounces), halved

- 1 **tablespoon extra-virgin olive oil**

Fleur del sel and freshly cracked black pepper

- 1 **head of radicchio—quartered, cored and leaves separated**
- 1 **head of butter lettuce, leaves torn into bite-size pieces**
- ⅓ **cup basil leaves**

Kosher salt

Humm created this salad for the opening menu at his Manhattan restaurant The NoMad, making as much as possible from scratch, including the lemon oil and apple cider vinegar. Because the recipe is so simple, he recommends high-quality ingredients: flavorful apples and the freshest mozzarella.

1. Make the marinated apples In a medium bowl, whisk the lemon juice with the olive oil and lemon oil and season with kosher salt. Add the apple and toss to coat.

2. Make the apple vinaigrette In a large bowl, whisk the apple cider vinegar with the olive oil, grapeseed oil, sugar and kosher salt.

3. Assemble the salad In a small bowl, toss the mozzarella with the olive oil and season with fleur de sel and freshly cracked black pepper. Add the radicchio, butter lettuce and basil to the apple vinaigrette, season with kosher salt and toss to coat. Arrange the greens on 4 plates, top with the marinated apples and mozzarella and serve.

MAKE AHEAD The apple vinaigrette can be refrigerated overnight.

For more on Daniel Humm & Will Guidara
Eleven Madison Park
@wguidara

POTATO-STUFFED
ROAST CHICKEN, P.136

SMOKE & PICKLES

Recipes & Stories from a New Southern Kitchen

BY **EDWARD LEE**

GRITS and rice porridge. Chowchow and kimchi. When Edward Lee moved to Louisville, Kentucky, more than a decade ago, he was struck by the similarities between Southern cooking and the food of his grandmother's native Korea. Lee, chef and co-owner of Louisville's acclaimed 610 Magnolia and a onetime contestant on Bravo's *Top Chef*, devotes his first cookbook to two fundamentals of both Southern and Korean cuisines: smoke (which he calls the "sixth flavor," after umami) and pickles. Sometimes he approaches them separately, but his charred T-bone steak with lemongrass and habanero (page 140) and squid salad with bacon, apple and ginger (page 138) show how beautifully smoky and tangy flavors go together.

Published by Artisan, $30

POTATO-STUFFED ROAST CHICKEN

Feeds **4 as a main course**

1 large Yukon Gold potato (about 11 ounces), peeled

1 tablespoon unsalted butter

2½ teaspoons kosher salt

¾ teaspoon freshly ground black pepper

One 3- to 3½-pound roasting chicken

2 teaspoons olive oil

Author's Note Once you've tried this recipe, you'll make it again and again. I promise. To vary the recipe, add about a teaspoon of chopped fresh rosemary or thyme to the potatoes while cooking them.

The perfect roasted chicken had always eluded me. There's no way to cook the thighs through without drying out the breast. I had gone through all the recipes I could try, but I'd never quite felt satisfied with any of them. Then I started trying out the technique in this recipe in the privacy of my home kitchen. It makes sense: the potatoes insulate the breasts, the fat from the skin flavors the potatoes, and the breasts stay incredibly moist. And the potatoes become an extra component without any more work. I've made this recipe twenty different ways, and this is my favorite. It's so easy you could do it in your sleep the second time around. My latest adjustment is to skip trussing the legs. The chicken may look a bit obscene when done, but allowing the legs to remain free allows more air to circulate around the thighs so the skin gets crispier and the meat cooks faster, in perfectly paced harmony with the insulated breasts.

1. Using the large holes of a box grater, grate the potato onto a cutting board. Wrap the grated potato in a square of cheesecloth and wring out as much water as possible.

2. Melt the butter in a large cast-iron skillet over medium heat. Add the grated potatoes, season with ½ teaspoon of the salt and ¼ teaspoon of the pepper, stir gently with a wooden spoon, and cook for exactly 2 minutes, no longer. Quickly transfer the potatoes to a plate and let cool.

3. Position a rack in the upper third of the oven and preheat the oven to 400°F.

4. Place the chicken on your work surface with the legs facing you. Starting at the tail end of each breast, use your fingers to gently loosen the skin from the flesh. Slide one finger in between the breast meat and the skin and move it from side to side to release the skin from the meat. Yes, this will feel funny, but carry on. Be careful not to tear the skin, but if it does rip a little, don't worry; it's not the end of the world. Rotate the bird so the breasts are now facing you and do the same thing starting at the neck end of the breasts, so that all of the breast skin is released from the meat.

5. Gently stuff the cooled potatoes into the space between the skin and breasts: Stuff half of them from the top and the remaining potatoes from the bottom. Now even out the potato layer: Place both your hands over the skin of the breasts and massage it to smooth and flatten the potatoes into an even layer. Rub the chicken with the olive oil and season with the remaining 2 teaspoons salt and ½ teaspoon pepper.

6. Wipe out the cast-iron skillet with a paper towel and heat it over medium heat. Place the chicken breast side down in the hot skillet, press it gently against the bottom of the pan, and hold it there for a bit while it browns lightly, about 3 minutes. Gently flip the chicken onto its back; the skin on top should be lightly browned. Slide the skillet into the oven and cook for 50 minutes to 1 hour. To check for doneness, insert an instant-read thermometer into the upper part of a thigh. I like my chicken when the thigh meat is at 155°F, but you may want yours at 160°F if you don't like any pink at all. Allow the chicken to rest in the pan for 10 minutes.

7. Transfer the chicken to a cutting board. Cut each breast away from the bones, being careful not to disturb the potatoes under the crispy skin. Slice each breast into 3 chunks and arrange on a platter. Carve the legs and add them to the platter, along with the wings.

QUICK-SAUTÉED SQUID & BACON SALAD WITH GRATED GINGER & APPLE

Feeds **4**

TAHINI VINAIGRETTE

- 2 **tablespoons tahini**
- 2 **tablespoons Asian sesame oil**
- 3 **tablespoons water**
- 1 **tablespoon sherry vinegar**
- 1 **tablespoon fresh lemon juice**
- **Salt and freshly ground black pepper**

- 8 **ounces bacon, cut into ½-inch-wide strips**
- 8 **cleaned squid, sliced into thin rings (see Author's Note)**
- 1 **teaspoon soy sauce**
- ½ **teaspoon fresh lemon juice**
- ¼ **teaspoon sea salt**
- **Dash of freshly ground black pepper**

GARNISH

- 1 **Granny Smith apple**
- 2 **teaspoons grated fresh ginger (use a Microplane)**
- 1 **bunch arugula**

Author's Note Make sure your squid is super-fresh. Don't buy frozen. The trick here is to cook the squid hot and fast. Longer cooking will cause the squid to turn rubbery, so make sure all your ingredients and plates are ready to go before you heat up the pan.

Author's Wine Choice
Serve with a Riesling.

There's a lot going on in this salad, but it's all very well balanced. Squid has a wonderful texture when it is sautéed quickly, but it can get rubbery very fast, so watch the timing carefully. It is almost still raw, just a little warmed up–kiss it on the heat, as we chefs like to say. Squid can be bland, though, so it needs a strong supporting cast. Bacon is always good for that, and the combination of fresh ginger and raw apple adds a spicy tart note that brightens up the entire dish.

1. To make the vinaigrette Combine the tahini, sesame oil, water, vinegar, and lemon juice in a blender and blend on high until well combined. Season with salt and pepper to taste. Transfer to a jar or small bowl.

2. Heat a large 10-inch skillet over medium heat. Add the bacon and sauté for 5 minutes, or until it is slightly crispy and most of the fat has rendered out. Transfer to a paper towel to drain, then transfer to a bowl.

3. Remove all but 2 teaspoons of the bacon fat from the skillet. Heat the remaining fat over medium-high heat. Add the squid and sauté, stirring constantly, for 2 minutes. Add the soy sauce, lemon juice, salt, and pepper and sauté for another minute, then immediately remove the squid from the pan and add to the bacon.

4. Using a Microplane, grate about half of the Granny Smith apple into a bowl, avoiding the core. Mix 2 tablespoons of the grated apple with the grated ginger. (I make this toward the end so that the freshly grated apple doesn't oxidize and turn brown.)

5. To serve, place a small bunch of arugula in the bottom of each of four shallow bowls. Place the squid mix over the arugula. Spoon about a tablespoon of the tahini vinaigrette over the squid in each bowl, spoon a little of the apple-ginger mixture over the squid, and serve immediately.

T-BONE STEAK WITH LEMONGRASS-HABANERO MARINADE

Feeds **4 normal people or 2 very hungry ones**

MARINADE

- **6 garlic cloves**
- **3 lemongrass stalks, trimmed to within 2 inches of the root end and finely minced**
- **2 habanero peppers, halved and seeds removed**

Juice of 1 lemon

Juice of 1 orange

- **2 tablespoons Asian sesame oil**
- **1 teaspoon soy sauce**
- **½ teaspoon salt**

Salt and freshly ground black pepper

Two 10-ounce T-bone steaks, ¾ inch thick (see Author's Note)

- **1 tablespoon unsalted butter**
- **1 teaspoon peanut oil**

Author's Note A T-bone steak is a decadent cut. You can easily substitute 8-ounce rib-eye or tenderloin steaks. Or, try this with sirloin cut into thin strips and stir-fried, using the remaining marinade to deglaze the pan.

Author's Beer Choice Serve with a glass of Circus Boy from Magic Hat Brewing.

Every once in a while, I like to dig into a big, fat, bloody steak. I might feel terrible the next day, but it's so tasty when I'm eating it. One problem I find with a big steak is that after a few bites, it starts to taste dull. So I like to add a bright acidic marinade for a contrast with all that meatiness. The acid actually accentuates the umami element in the steak and gives it a punch that is quite addictive.

1. To make the marinade Combine all the ingredients in a blender and blitz on high until well blended.

2. Generously salt and pepper the steaks. Place in a glass baking dish and pour half of the marinade over the steaks. Marinate at room temperature for 20 minutes.

3. In a large cast-iron skillet, heat the butter and peanut oil over high heat until just barely smoking. Add the steaks, cover the pan with a lid, and cook for 3 minutes. Uncover, flip the steaks, and reduce the heat to medium. Cook the steaks, uncovered, for another 2 minutes or so. Do the steaks look caramelized and moist and shiny from the marinade? Good, they are ready to eat. Remove the steaks from the pan and let rest on a cutting board for 2 minutes.

4. Spoon the pan juices over the steaks; serve immediately.

"From the sizzling Korean grills of my childhood to the barbeque culture of the South, I've always lived where food was wrapped in a blanket of smokiness." *–Ed Lee*

ROASTED OKRA & CAULIFLOWER SALAD

Feeds **6 to 8 as a side dish**

½ head (about 10 ounces) cauliflower, cut into small florets

8 ounces okra, trimmed (see Author's Note) and halved lengthwise

2 teaspoons olive oil

1½ teaspoons ground cumin

1 teaspoon salt

5 dried apricots, thinly sliced

¼ cup chopped roasted cashews

Grated zest of 1 orange (1 teaspoon)

Juice of ½ orange

Author's Note Make this during the height of okra season, late spring to summer. Pick small, tender okra; when okra is young and fresh, there's no need to trim the tops—they are soft enough to eat.

Don't be put off by what you've heard about the sliminess of okra. That "slime," which is actually called mucilage, covers the seed pods and is released when the okra is cut into. Roasting okra in the dry high heat of your oven renders it tender while minimizing the mucilage. The cumin here gives the okra and cauliflower a spicy floral note, which is balanced by the sweetness of the dried apricots.

1. Preheat the oven to 400°F.

2. Place the cauliflower on one baking sheet and the okra on another. Drizzle 1 teaspoon of the olive oil over the cauliflower, sprinkle with ¾ teaspoon of the cumin and ½ teaspoon of the salt, and toss well. Repeat with the okra and the remaining 1 teaspoon oil, ¾ teaspoon cumin, and ½ teaspoon salt. Spread out the cauliflower and okra.

3. Place both pans in the oven and bake the okra for about 10 minutes, the cauliflower for about 25 minutes. They are done when they are soft, slightly shriveled, and just a little browned around the edges. Transfer the okra to a large bowl, then add the cauliflower when it is done.

4. Add the dried apricots, cashews, orange zest, and juice and toss well. (The salad can be kept warm in a 200°F oven until ready to eat.)

5. Serve in warm bowls.

CREAMY SAUERKRAUT SOUP

Total **45 min**
Serves **6**

5 tablespoons unsalted butter

3 ounces bacon, chopped (½ cup)

1 small onion, finely chopped (1 cup)

10 ounces drained and lightly rinsed sauerkraut (3 cups)

¾ cup dry white wine

5 cups chicken stock or low-sodium broth

½ cup heavy cream

4 teaspoons sour cream

2 teaspoons Dijon mustard

Kosher salt and pepper

Baby arugula leaves, for garnish

Lee created this smooth, velvety soup using mason jars of sauerkraut canned by his German in-laws. He purees the soup with a little cream to mellow the sharpness of the sauerkraut. The result is hearty, tangy and deeply satisfying.

1. In a medium pot, melt 2 tablespoons of the butter. Add the bacon and onion and cook over moderate heat, stirring occasionally, until the bacon is browned and crisp, about 5 minutes. Add the sauerkraut and wine and cook until most of the liquid is absorbed, 4 to 5 minutes. Stir in the stock and cream and bring to a simmer. Simmer gently until slightly reduced and the flavors meld, about 20 minutes. Remove from the heat and stir in the sour cream, mustard and the remaining 3 tablespoons of butter.

2. Working in 2 batches, transfer the soup to a blender and puree until smooth. Season with salt and pepper. Ladle the soup into 6 bowls and garnish with arugula.

SERVE WITH Warm biscuits and sausages.

For more on Edward Lee
chefedwardlee.com
Chef Edward Lee
@chefedwardlee

VANILLA-CINNAMON
CHIA PUDDING
PARFAITS, P.146

EXOTIC TABLE

Flavors, Inspiration & Recipes from Around the World–to Your Kitchen

BY **ALIYA LEEKONG**

IN a cookbook title, "exotic" might indicate complicated recipes with challenging flavors. But Aliya LeeKong, chef at the Michelin-starred Indian restaurant Junoon in New York City, makes the exotic accessible. In her first cookbook, she calls for spices and other high-impact flavors from all over the world, with some of those ingredients reflecting her personal history–her family is Indo-Pakistani and Tanzanian. Each recipe has its secret weapon: For Korean-style BBQ chicken (page 148), it's *gochujang*, a chile sauce that balances sweetness and heat; for sugar and spice pecans (page 150), it's North African *ras el hanout*. LeeKong's red lentil pâté (page 147) shows her particular affinity for the Indian spices she's been using (and taming) since childhood.

Published by Adams Media, $35

VANILLA-CINNAMON CHIA PUDDING PARFAIT

Vegetarian, gluten-free
Yields **4 to 6 servings**

½ cup chia seeds

½ teaspoon ground cinnamon

2¼ cups regular, low-fat,
   or almond milk

 1 teaspoon vanilla extract

 1 tablespoon honey

½ cup sliced almonds, toasted

1½ cups mixed berries

Chia seeds have worked their way into my morning ritual, and this is one of the many ways I enjoy them. They're a superfood, native to parts of Mexico and Guatemala, and are amazing in this "pudding parfait." The little seeds can hold 9 to 12 times their weight in liquid, so when added to water or milk here, they swell up, become gelatinous, and take on a pudding-like texture. With hints of vanilla and cinnamon and layered with fresh fruit and toasted nuts, this is a great way to start the day.

1. In a medium bowl, add the chia and the cinnamon. Pour in the milk, whisking to make sure the chia doesn't clump and the cinnamon mixes in thoroughly.

2. Add the vanilla and honey and whisk to combine. Chill for a minimum of 30 minutes.

3. Layer the pudding over the nuts and berries and top with both. Serve chilled.

NOTE Chia acts as a complete protein, has more calcium than skim milk on a per-ounce basis, and is the richest plant source of omega-3.

RED LENTIL PÂTÉ WITH TOASTED CASHEWS & INDIAN SPICES

Vegan
Yields **approximately 2½ cups**

- 1 **cup red split lentils, picked through and rinsed**
- 2 **cups water**
- ½ **teaspoon turmeric**
- 2 to 3 **tablespoons canola oil**
- ½ **teaspoon white cumin seeds**
- 1 **large shallot, finely chopped**
- 1 **jalapeño or Thai green chili, finely chopped**
- ½ **teaspoon minced ginger**
- ½ **teaspoon ground cumin**
- ½ **teaspoon ground coriander**
- **Pinch cayenne pepper**
- 4 to 5 **garlic cloves, minced**
- 1 **tomato, seeded, strained of juice, and chopped**
- ⅓ **cup raw cashews, toasted**
- **Freshly squeezed lemon juice, to taste**
- **Salt, to taste**
- **Small handful of cilantro, finely chopped**
- **Crusty bread or crackers, for serving**

When I'm entertaining, I like to serve a vegetarian pâté like this one—it more than makes up for in flavor what it lacks in fat (like a liver pâté). The inspiration for this is daal, a rich, South Asian lentil dish. Sweet red lentils, tons of fragrant spices, along with aromatics like shallots, chili, garlic, and ginger, make this pâté an unusual but welcome change from the traditional.

1. In a medium saucepan, bring lentils with water and turmeric up to a rolling boil over medium-high heat and cook for 10 minutes uncovered. Watch that it's not boiling too hard as it can easily boil over. Skim off any scum as it comes to the top during this period and then cover and cook another 15 to 20 minutes, until lentils are completely soft and can be mashed. Set aside to cool.

2. Heat a medium skillet over medium heat. Add the oil and the cumin seeds. When they start to sputter (after a minute or so), add the shallots, chili, and ginger and sauté for 3 to 4 minutes, until the shallots are translucent. Add the spices and garlic and sauté for another 30 seconds to a minute, until fragrant. Add the tomatoes and cook until the tomatoes break down and can be mashed. Set aside to cool.

3. Transfer the lentils and the shallot mixture to the bowl of a food processor. Add the raw cashews, a squeeze of lemon juice, and season with salt. Process until the mixture is uniform. Adjust seasoning (it can take quite a bit of salt) and lemon juice to taste.

4. Transfer to a container and refrigerate until completely cooled.

5. Serve garnished with some chopped cilantro and with crusty bread or crackers.

KOREAN-STYLE BBQ CHICKEN OR TURKEY DRUMSTICKS

Serves **4 to 6**

10 to 12 chicken drumsticks (approximately 3 pounds), or 5 to 6 small turkey drumsticks

1 tablespoon gochujang, sriracha, or other chili sauce (see Note)

4 to 6 garlic cloves, minced

½ teaspoon minced ginger

1 tablespoon mirin

½ cup low-sodium soy sauce

1 tablespoon sesame oil

2 teaspoons honey

Toasted sesame seeds, to garnish

Editor's Beer Choice
Lively, spiced Belgian-style wheat ale: Allagash White

These drumsticks are inspired by Korean barbecue—that perfect blend of sweet, salty, spicy, and umami. For that signature flavor, I use gochujang, a sweet Korean chili sauce, which adds just the right heat here, but you can use another chili sauce like sriracha and still get great results. Easy to do in the oven, these require nothing more than a dip in a marinade that doubles as a glaze and some cook time. Cooking outdoors? These taste even better on the grill . . . .

1. Place the chicken in a plastic bag and add the chili sauce, garlic, ginger, mirin, soy sauce, sesame oil, and honey. Close and turn to distribute the ingredients evenly. Marinate for a minimum of 6 hours or overnight.

2. Preheat the oven to 450°F.

3. Remove the drumsticks from the marinade, reserving the marinade, and wipe them dry. Place them on a baking sheet fitted with a rack and let them come up to room temperature. Place in the oven and drop the temperature to 375°F. Roast for 35 minutes for the chicken drumsticks, longer for the turkey, so that a thermometer registers 165°F when inserted.

4. While the drumsticks are cooking, strain the marinade into a saucepan. Bring up to a boil and reduce to a simmer. Simmer uncovered for 5 to 10 minutes, until the sauce coats a spoon and becomes a bit syrupy.

5. Serve drumsticks hot, brushed with the soy glaze and sprinkled with the toasted sesame seeds.

NOTE If you are using a chili sauce other than gochujang, bump up the sweetness a bit—add another teaspoon of honey.

SUGAR & SPICE PECANS

Vegetarian, gluten-free
Yields **approximately 4 cups**

- 4 **tablespoons unsalted butter**
- ¼ **cup honey**
- 4 **teaspoons light brown sugar**
- 2 **tablespoons Ras El Hanout (see Note; recipe follows)**
- 1 **teaspoon salt**
- 1 **pound pecan halves**

These party snacks whip up in no time–toasted pecans, lightly caramelized and scented with a beautiful North African spice blend. I put these out next to my cheese plate and watch as they get inhaled. They have just the right touch of sweetness balanced with a salty, buttery warm spiciness that is irresistible. The best part? The leftover pecans can easily be tossed into a simple salad to dress it right up.

1. Preheat the oven to 300°F.

2. In a skillet, melt the butter with the honey, sugar, Ras El Hanout, and salt over medium-low heat, whisking to dissolve the spices. Once it's a uniform consistency, remove from the heat, add the pecans, and toss to coat thoroughly.

3. Transfer the pecans to a parchment-lined baking sheet and spread out to create a single layer. Bake for 20 to 25 minutes.

4. Let cool before serving. The sugar and spice coating will harden up a bit and give it a nice crunch. Store them in an airtight container. At room temperature, they should keep for 2 to 3 weeks and in the freezer for much longer.

NOTE Ras El Hanout is a gorgeous, North African spice blend. You can use my personal blend [on page 152] or find the spice blend at an ethnic grocer. If you are using another blend besides mine, please pay attention to the salt and adjust up or down accordingly in this recipe.

continued on page 152

A fragrant
North African
spice mix
transforms
roasted nuts.

SUGAR & SPICE PECANS *continued*

Vegan
Yields **1 scant cup**

¼ cup white cumin seeds

¼ cup sweet paprika

¼ cup ground black pepper

1 tablespoon ground cinnamon

2 teaspoons ground ginger

1½ teaspoons turmeric

1 teaspoon cayenne pepper

Large pinch saffron

1 teaspoon salt

Ras El Hanout

This North African blend is another staple I always have on hand in my exotic pantry. Ras El Hanout quite literally means "top of the shop" and is supposed to represent the most coveted blend the spice merchant has to offer, but I like to think of it as a Moroccan curry. The flavor is nuanced and complex, a heady mixture that's difficult to describe. It tastes to me like the smell of walking into a spice shop! My shortened blend is an easy one and is great on weeknight chicken thighs, to jazz up some plain rice, or on roasted potatoes.

1. In a small skillet, toast the cumin seeds over medium heat until they deepen in color and turn fragrant, about 3 to 5 minutes. Grind to a fine powder using a spice or coffee grinder.

2. Combine the ground, roasted cumin with the remaining ingredients.

3. Store in an airtight container—the blend should keep up to 3 months.

NOTE There are countless variations of this North African specialty and each shop, family, and region has its own list of ingredients, sometimes reaching upwards of 40 spices! Rosebuds may be added for a floral touch, grains of paradise for a peppery note, lavender for aromatic purposes. Some spice merchants go so far as to add spices, herbs, or other extractions that have aphrodisiacal effects . . . clearly trying to get repeat customers!

YUZU-GLAZED BROWN BUTTER MADELEINES

Active **40 min**; Total **2 hr**
Makes **3 dozen madeleines**

MADELEINES

- 1 **stick plus 2 tablespoons unsalted butter, plus more for greasing the molds**
- 1¼ **cups all-purpose flour, plus more for dusting the molds**
- 1 **teaspoon baking powder**
- 1 **teaspoon kosher salt**
- ⅔ **cup granulated sugar**
- **Finely grated zest of 1 lemon**
- 4 **large eggs, at room temperature**
- 1½ **teaspoons pure vanilla extract**

YUZU GLAZE

- 1 **cup confectioners' sugar**
- 1½ **tablespoons yuzu juice**

"Yuzu and brown butter take ordinary madeleines to another level," LeeKong says. While classic madeleines are scented with lemon, she coats the little cakes with a silky glaze made with yuzu, an Asian citrus with hints of grapefruit, mandarin orange and lime.

1. Make the madeleines In a small saucepan, melt the butter. Cook over moderately low heat until deep golden and nutty-smelling, 5 to 7 minutes. Strain the browned butter through a cheesecloth-lined sieve into a small bowl. Let cool completely.

2. In a medium bowl, sift the flour with the baking powder and salt. In another medium bowl, using a handheld electric mixer at medium speed, beat the granulated sugar with the lemon zest until well combined. Add the eggs and beat at high speed until they have tripled in volume and form ribbons when the beater is lifted, about 10 minutes. Beat in the vanilla, then gently fold in the dry ingredients. Gently whisk ⅓ cup of the batter into the browned butter until smooth, then fold the butter mixture back into the batter. Cover and refrigerate the batter for at least 1 hour.

3. Generously brush 36 madeleine molds with butter, then dust with flour, shaking off the excess. Refrigerate the molds.

4. Preheat the oven to 375°F and position a rack in the middle of the oven. Spoon heaping tablespoonfuls of the batter into the center of the prepared madeleine molds (do not spread the batter to fill the molds) and bake for 11 to 13 minutes, until the edges are golden and the cakes spring back when pressed lightly. Transfer the molds to a rack to let the madeleines cool completely, then tap them out onto the rack.

5. Meanwhile, make the glaze In a medium bowl, whisk the confectioners' sugar with the yuzu juice and 1 tablespoon of water until smooth. Dip the cooled madeleines in the glaze and transfer to a rack until the glaze sets, about 10 minutes, then serve.

For more on Aliya LeeKong
aliyaleekong.com
 Aliya LeeKong
 @aliyaleekong

Deborah Madison grows Bright Lights Swiss chard in her garden in Galisteo, New Mexico.

VEGETABLE LITERACY

Cooking & Gardening with Twelve Families from the Edible Plant Kingdom, with over 300 Deliciously Simple Recipes

BY **DEBORAH MADISON**

HERE'S the new vegetable bible. Deborah Madison, who got her start at Chez Panisse in Berkeley over three decades ago and went on to open the groundbreaking vegetarian restaurant Greens in San Francisco, has written nearly a dozen vegetable-driven cookbooks, but her latest is by far her most comprehensive. In addition to deep notes on botany and nutrition, she writes enticing recipes with helpful variations. She says she's never made her wilted red cabbage with goat feta (page 156) the same way twice, and suggests a slew of different herbs and flavorings for readers to try. Her fresh tomato and celery salad with avocado (page 160) can be served as a side or a taco filling. Madison's tips on swaps, substitutions and alternative uses make for smarter cooking.

Published by Ten Speed Press, $40

WILTED RED CABBAGE WITH MINT & GOAT FETA

For **2 to 4**

2 tablespoons olive oil

1 medium red onion, quartered through the stem end and thinly sliced crosswise

1 garlic clove, finely chopped

4 cups packed very finely sliced red cabbage (a scant pound)

Sea salt

Juice of 1 lemon

2 tablespoons chopped mint

2 tablespoons chopped dill

2 tablespoons finely chopped parsley

Freshly ground pepper

Crumbled goat feta plus whole mint leaves, to finish

I prefer a lightly wilted, warm red cabbage salad to the same vegetable uncooked for its lush color and more tender texture. The thinner you slice the cabbage, the more tender it will be. A mandoline is a good tool to use here, or a very sharp knife.

I don't think I've made this the same way ever. Cabbage is so compatible with herbs and seeds of all kinds, from fennel greens to fragrant dill to caraway seeds, lovage to marjoram, olive to sesame.

Heat the oil in a large skillet or wok. When hot, add the onion, turn to coat it with the oil, and cook for a minute to sear and soften. Add the garlic, then the cabbage, and season with 1 teaspoon salt. Immediately begin turning it in the pan to wilt it evenly. You don't want to fully cook it, just wilt it; two minutes should be enough time. Remove the pan from the heat, toss the cabbage with 2 tablespoons of the lemon juice, then taste and add more if sharpness is desired. Toss with the herbs. Season with more salt, if needed, and plenty of pepper. Transfer the cabbage to a platter, mounding it in a heap, then shower with the crumbled goat feta. Finish with the extra mint leaves and serve.

HALLOUMI WITH SEARED RED PEPPERS, OLIVES & CAPERS

For **2 as a main course**
or **4 as a first course**

Large handful of halved or quartered cherry or other fruit tomatoes

12 Kalamata olives, pitted and halved

1 large clove garlic, minced

2 tablespoons capers, rinsed

3 tablespoons olive oil

6 pimientos or 2 red, yellow, or orange bell peppers, seeded and cut lengthwise into ½-inch-wide strips

8 slices halloumi cheese (8 ounces), ½ inch thick

1 tablespoon chopped mint

1 tablespoon chopped parsley

Sea salt and freshly ground pepper

Warm crusty country bread or pita bread, for serving

Editor's Wine Choice Medium-bodied, red cherry–scented Greek red: 2011 Domaine Skouras Saint George Nemea

Emily Swantner, a traveler and cook with a pop-up supper club, served this at one of her dinners. She uses sun-dried tomatoes, but I prefer fresh, so take your choice. I'm nuts about halloumi, that durable white cheese from Cyprus that you can sauté or grill. Smother it with seared late-summer peppers and nothing is better.

Combine the tomatoes, olives, garlic, and capers in a bowl and moisten with 4 teaspoons of the olive oil.

Heat 1 tablespoon of the oil in a skillet over high heat. When the oil is hot, add the peppers and sauté until softened and seared, 3 to 4 minutes. Add them to the bowl.

Return the pan to medium-high heat and add the remaining 2 teaspoons oil. When the oil is hot, add the cheese and cook, turning to color both sides golden. This takes only a few minutes. Return the pepper mixture to the pan and cook for about 1 minute, then turn off the heat and add the mint and parsley. Season with salt and pepper. Serve sizzling from the pan with the warm bread.

WITH SALAD Add crisp, undressed salad greens and a spoonful of *harissa* to each plate.

WITH FRYING PEPPERS Instead of the meaty bells or pimientos, use any of the frying peppers. They won't need to cook quite as long as the others to soften.

TOMATO & CELERY SALAD WITH CUMIN, CILANTRO & AVOCADO

For **4**

- 2 celery stalks, peeled if stringy and finely diced
- About 2 cups assorted small fruit-type tomatoes, halved or quartered
- 1 shallot, diced
- 2 tablespoons olive oil
- 1 tablespoon lemon juice
- ½ teaspoon cumin seeds, toasted and ground
- 1 tablespoon finely chopped cilantro, plus sprigs to finish
- 1 tablespoon finely slivered celery leaves
- Sea salt and freshly ground pepper
- 1 large avocado

Of course, tomatoes are wonderful with basil, but I also like them with cumin, celery, cilantro, and avocado chunks. This salad is a good side to grilled lamb chops or a great filling for tacos or quesadillas.

Put the diced celery, tomatoes, and shallot in a wide bowl. In a small bowl, whisk together the oil, lemon juice, cumin, cilantro, and celery leaves. Pour the dressing over the tomatoes and turn gently with a rubber spatula. Season with a few pinches of salt and plenty of pepper.

Halve, pit, and peel the avocado, then slice into wide wedges and cut each wedge in half crosswise. Add the avocado to the tomatoes and gently fold it in. Finish with the cilantro sprigs and serve.

CHERRY GRATIN WITH FRANGIPANE

Active **30 min;** Total **1 hr 30 min**
Serves **6**

9 tablespoons unsalted butter, softened, plus more for greasing the baking dish

2 pounds fresh cherries, stemmed and pitted

2 tablespoons granulated sugar

1 tablespoon plus ¼ teaspoon kirsch

1½ cups almond meal

3 large eggs

3 tablespoons heavy cream

1½ cups confectioners' sugar, plus more for dusting

¾ teaspoon pure almond extract

For her homey, warm gratin, Madison bakes ripe fruit under a blanket of frangipane (a smooth almond custard). She uses cherries here but says that any kind of fruit is marvelous: "Plums, apricots and cherries are my favorites for early summer; prune plums and peaches a month or two later; pears for late fall."

1. Preheat the oven to 375°F. Butter a 2-quart heatproof baking dish.

2. In a large skillet, combine the cherries, granulated sugar and 1 tablespoon of the kirsch. Cook over moderately low heat, stirring, until the sugar is dissolved, about 5 minutes. Scrape the cherries and juices into the prepared baking dish.

3. In a large bowl, using a handheld electric mixer, beat the almond meal with the 9 tablespoons of butter at medium speed until well incorporated, about 2 minutes. Add the eggs, cream and the 1½ cups of confectioners' sugar and beat until thick, smooth and well blended, about 2 minutes. Beat in the remaining ¼ teaspoon of kirsch and the almond extract. Spread the frangipane evenly over the cherries.

4. Bake the gratin for about 40 minutes, until golden and set. Transfer to a rack to cool until warm. Dust lightly with confectioners' sugar and serve warm or at room temperature.

MAKE AHEAD The baked gratin can stand at room temperature for up to 2 hours.

**For more on
Deborah Madison**

deborahmadison.com
🅕 Deborah Madison

SPANISH FLAVORS

Stunning Dishes Inspired by the Regional Ingredients of Spain

BY **JOSÉ PIZARRO**

LONDON chef José Pizarro (at left in center) couldn't decide which region of his native Spain would be the focus of his next cookbook, so after a couple of glasses of Txakoli at a bar in San Sebastián, he decided to feature all of them. Here, Pizarro tweaks traditional dishes: He describes the centuries-old way some tuna is still caught off Spain's southern coast, then offers his recipe for seared tuna steak with a salsa verde to which he adds olives for extra flavor (page 170). In a chapter devoted to the islands, he offers a vibrant, vinegary squid with potatoes (page 166) that's his take on the classic Spanish tapa *calamari a la romana* (deep-fried squid), except he sautés his version to preserve more squid taste. All these dishes show that Pizarro approaches Spanish cuisine respectfully, but with originality.

Published by Kyle Books, $30

BROILED FIGS WITH GOAT CHEESE, HONEY & WALNUTS

Serves **4**

Heaping ⅓ cup walnut pieces

8 large fresh figs

3½ ounces rindless goat cheese, thinly sliced

3 tablespoons honey

4 large mint leaves, finely shredded

Editor's Wine Choice
Cherry-inflected Spanish sparkling wine: 2010 Llopart Reserva Brut Rosé Cava

This recipe reminds me of my father, because he has figs and walnuts in his garden and makes honey. We used to get goat curd from the local farmer, which was so delicious. Now it is harder to get, so I have used a soft goat cheese instead.

Preheat the broiler to medium-high. Spread the walnuts on a baking sheet and carefully toast them for a minute or two until lightly golden. Remove, and leave to go cold.

Cut a deep cross into the top of each fig, about two-thirds of the way down to the base, and then give them a gentle squeeze, to open them up slightly like a flower. Divide the goat cheese evenly between each fig, and place them on a baking sheet. Broil for 3 to 4 minutes until the figs are soft, and the cheese is bubbling and lightly golden.

Lift the figs onto plates and drizzle a little honey over each one. Sprinkle with the walnuts and mint before serving.

SAUTÉED SQUID, ONIONS & POTATOES WITH CHILI PEPPER & SHERRY VINEGAR

Serves **4**

⅓ cup extra-virgin olive oil

1 medium onion, halved and thinly sliced

9 ounces small waxy potatoes, such as Charlotte, unpeeled

1 pound medium squid, cleaned

½ teaspoon crushed dried red pepper flakes

1 garlic clove, finely chopped

Leaves from 2 large fresh thyme sprigs

1 tablespoon sherry vinegar

1 tablespoon chopped flat-leaf parsley

Sea salt and freshly ground black pepper

Editor's Wine Choice Zesty
Albariño: 2012 La Cana

This recipe is amazing. I love *calamari a la romana* (deep-fried squid), one of the most popular tapas all over Spain, and synonymous with Spanish cooking, but I think calamari deserves more than that. This is one great example. The most important thing is to caramelize the onions well, so take your time.

Heat 2 tablespoons of the oil in a large frying pan, add the onion, cover, and cook over medium-low heat, stirring occasionally, for about 15 minutes until it is soft, and nicely caramelized. Meanwhile, cook the potatoes in salted boiling water for 15 minutes until tender. Drain, peel and cut in half lengthwise.

Slice the squid pouches crosswise into ¼-inch-thick rings. Leave the tentacles as they are.

Heat another tablespoon of the oil in a small frying pan and add the potatoes, cut-side down. Fry gently for 2 to 3 minutes, turning them over halfway through, until crisp and nicely golden. Set aside over very low heat.

Heat another tablespoon of the oil in a large frying pan, add half the squid and half the red pepper flakes, season with salt, and fry over high heat for 1½ minutes, adding half the garlic halfway through, until the squid is cooked and nicely caramelized. Transfer to the small frying pan with the potatoes to keep warm, and fry the rest of the squid as before with the remaining oil, red pepper flakes, and garlic. Return the first batch of squid, along with the potatoes, to the large pan, sprinkle in the thyme leaves and toss together briefly over medium-high heat to mix them together. Drizzle in the sherry vinegar, add the chopped parsley and caramelized onion, toss together once more, and serve.

PASTA WITH CHORIZO & MUSSELS

Serves **4**

6 tablespoons extra-virgin olive oil

3 garlic cloves, finely chopped

½ teaspoon crushed dried red pepper flakes

14 ounces skinned, chopped tomatoes, fresh or canned

2¼ pounds fresh mussels

14 ounces dried spaghetti

6 tablespoons dry white wine

7 ounces cooking chorizo sausage, skinned and diced

2 tablespoons chopped flat-leaf parsley

Sea salt and freshly ground black pepper

Editor's Wine Choice Spicy, robust Priorat red: 2012 Alvaro Palacios Camins del Priorat

Pasta is popular in the east of Spain. You might wonder why a Spanish chef is cooking with pasta, but so many Italian chefs are cooking wonderful dishes with chorizo, so why not? I created this dish with my friend Diego in Barcelona. I still remember buying the mussels from La Boqueria, the famous food market in that city, and marrying the flavors with a very nice glass of red wine from Priorat.

Put 4 tablespoons of the olive oil, the garlic, and dried red pepper flakes in a large frying pan or saucepan and place it over medium-high heat. As soon as the garlic is sizzling, add the tomatoes, and simmer gently for 15 minutes until well reduced, quite thick, and just starting to stick to the bottom of the pan.

Meanwhile, bring a large pan of salted water to a boil. Wash the mussels, pull out the beards from between the tightly closed shells, and discard any that are open, and won't close when tapped on a work surface. Add the spaghetti to the boiling water, and cook for 10 to 11 minutes, or until al punto—still with a little bite.

Heat another large pan over high heat, add the mussels and the wine, cover, and cook for 2 to 3 minutes, shaking the pan occasionally, until all the mussels are only just open. Take care not to overcook them at this stage. Pour them into a colander placed over a bowl to collect the cooking juices. Stir all but the last tablespoon or two of the cooking liquid into the tomato sauce, and continue to simmer until the sauce has reduced and thickened once more, but is a little more moist than before. Season to taste with salt and pepper. Remove half of the larger mussels from their shells.

Heat the remaining olive oil in a frying pan, add the chorizo, and fry gently for 1 minute until lightly golden. Drain the spaghetti, return to the pan, and add the tomato sauce, cooked mussels, chorizo sausage, and chopped parsley. Toss well together and serve.

Dried Spanish
chorizo
is best here.

SEARED TUNA STEAK WITH SALSA VERDE ON GRILLED POTATOES

Serves **4**

18 ounces small, evenly sized waxy new potatoes

1 tablespoon olive oil, plus extra for brushing

Sea salt and freshly ground black pepper

Four 7-ounce tuna steaks, cut 1¼ inches thick

FOR THE SALSA VERDE

⅓ cup each of flat-leaf parsley leaves, mint leaves and basil leaves

1 garlic clove, thinly sliced

2 tablespoons salted capers, rinsed well, drained, and dried

½ cup good-quality pitted green olives

4 anchovy fillets in oil

Finely grated zest of ¼ small lemon

1 teaspoon Dijon mustard

1½ tablespoons lemon juice

8 tablespoons extra-virgin olive oil

Editor's Wine Choice Ripe, red cherry–inflected Spanish rosé: 2013 Artazuri Rosado

The last time I was cooking for my great friend and photographer Emma Lee, I overcooked the tuna—I was chatting too much and forgot to check it, but she was happy and satisfied when I cooked this dish for her for this book! Adding olives to a salsa verde gives extra flavor and an oiliness, which complements the tuna. This recipe makes a generous amount of salsa verde, but it is also wonderful served with grilled steaks.

Cut the potatoes into ¼-inch-thick slices. Put them into a pan of salted cold water, bring to a boil, and simmer for 5 minutes, or until they are only just tender when pierced with the tip of a knife. Drain well, leave the steam to die down, then toss them with 1 tablespoon olive oil, and some salt and pepper.

For the salsa verde, drop the herbs into boiling water, leave for 5 seconds, then drain and refresh under cold water. Squeeze out all the excess water, then put onto a chopping board with the sliced garlic, capers, olives, and anchovies, and finely chop everything together. Scoop the mixture into a bowl, and stir in the lemon zest, mustard, lemon juice, olive oil, and some freshly ground black pepper.

Heat a cast-iron grill pan over high heat, then reduce the heat to medium. Add half the sliced potatoes in one layer, and grill for about 3 minutes on each side until golden. Transfer to a baking sheet, sprinkle with a little more salt, and keep hot in a low oven while you cook the remainder. Add them to the baking sheet and keep hot.

Brush the tuna steaks with oil and season. Return the cast-iron grill pan to high heat, and when it is smoking hot, reduce the heat to medium-high. Place the steaks side-by-side on the grill pan and cook for 1 to 1½ minutes on each side until nicely marked on the outside, but still rare in the center.

As you turn the tuna steaks over, divide the potatoes between 4 warmed plates. Put the tuna on top, spoon over some of the salsa verde, and serve.

Piquant olives
make the
salsa verde
extra-briny.

Boqueria market, Pizarro's first stop for breakfast in Barcelona.

CHICKEN FLAMENQUINES WITH SERRANO HAM, ROMESCO & ALLIOLI

Total **1 hr 10 min**
Serves **4**

ROMESCO

- 2 **medium tomatoes, halved crosswise**
- ¼ **cup hazelnuts**
- 2 **tablespoons extra-virgin olive oil**
- ¼ **cup blanched almonds**
- 1 **slice of white sandwich bread, crusts removed and bread diced**
- 1 **large garlic clove, crushed**
- 2 **chipotles in adobo, seeded**
- 1½ **teaspoons sherry vinegar**
- **Kosher salt and pepper**

ALLIOLI

- ¾ **cup mayonnaise**
- 1½ **teaspoons fresh lemon juice**
- 1 **small garlic clove, minced**
- **Kosher salt**

CHICKEN

- **Eight 4-ounce chicken cutlets, pounded ¼ inch thick**
- **Kosher salt and pepper**
- 8 **thin slices of serrano ham**
- 1½ **cups all-purpose flour**
- 2 **large eggs**
- 10 **ounces kettle-cooked potato chips, finely crushed**
- **Vegetable oil, for frying**

Editor's Wine Choice Fragrant, medium-bodied Spanish white: 2012 Telmo Rodríguez Basa

For more on José Pizarro
josepizarro.com
 @Jose_Pizarro

Traditional *flamenquines* are pork loins wrapped in serrano ham, then breaded and fried. Here, Pizarro uses chicken breasts, coating thin cutlets with crushed potato chips for an extra-crisp crust and serving them with fiery, nutty *romesco* and garlicky *allioli*. The amounts in the recipe ensure leftover sauces, which are also excellent with grilled fish, poultry, meats or vegetables.

1. Make the romesco Preheat a large cast-iron skillet. Add the tomatoes cut side down and cook over high heat, turning once, until lightly charred, about 6 minutes. Transfer to a food processor.

2. In the large skillet, toast the hazelnuts over moderate heat until the skins wrinkle, 5 minutes. Transfer to a clean kitchen towel and rub the skins off. In the same skillet, heat the oil. Add the hazelnuts and almonds and cook over moderate heat, stirring occasionally, until browned, 3 to 5 minutes. Add the bread and garlic; cook over moderately high heat, stirring, until golden, 2 minutes. Transfer the mixture to the food processor and let cool. Add the chipotles and vinegar and puree until nearly smooth. Season with salt and pepper; transfer the *romesco* to a medium bowl. Wipe out the skillet.

3. Make the allioli In another medium bowl, whisk the mayonnaise with the lemon juice and garlic and season with salt.

4. Prepare the chicken Season the chicken cutlets with salt and pepper and place 1 slice of ham on each. Starting at the narrow end, tightly roll up the cutlets and transfer to a baking sheet.

5. Spread the flour in a shallow bowl. In another shallow bowl, beat the eggs with a pinch each of salt and pepper. Spread the crushed chips in a third shallow bowl. Dredge the chicken rolls in the flour, tapping off the excess. Dip the coated rolls in the beaten egg, then dredge in the chips, lightly patting to help them adhere.

6. Set a rack over a baking sheet. In the large cast-iron skillet, heat ½ inch of vegetable oil to 350°F. Add the chicken rolls and fry over moderate heat, turning occasionally, until browned and an instant-read thermometer inserted in the center of each roll registers 165°F, about 17 minutes. Transfer the *flamenquines* to the rack to drain, then arrange on a platter and serve with the *romesco* and *allioli*.

For dinner parties, Diane Cu uses flowers, lemons and produce from her garden in Costa Mesa, California.

BOUNTIFUL

Recipes Inspired
by Our Garden

BY **TODD PORTER** AND **DIANE CU**

WHEN Todd Porter and Diane Cu met, their shared love of food nearly led them to open a restaurant. Instead, they started a blog, the archly named White on Rice Couple (he's from an Oregon cattle ranch, she's from Vietnam). Fans will recognize the couple's devotion to seasonal cooking in their new book, which revolves around their prolific Southern California backyard garden. The recipes are uncomplicated but inspired: tabouli with roasted corn (page 178), and a cucumber and mint quinoa salad dressed with rice vinegar and soy sauce (page 182). Even their lemon trees contribute, in the light, tangy lemon and cream spaghetti (page 180). It's the kind of cooking anyone with a garden–or a nearby farmers' market–can embrace.

Published by Stewart, Tabori & Chang, $35

ROASTED CHERRY TOMATO & GOAT CHEESE DIP

Serves **4 to 6**

3 tablespoons olive oil

½ pound (225 grams) cherry tomatoes

1 cup (240 ml) whole-milk ricotta

1 medium clove garlic, minced

¼ cup (15 grams) minced fresh flat-leaf parsley

¼ teaspoon salt

Zest of 1 lemon

½ teaspoon fresh lemon juice

One 8-ounce/225-gram log goat cheese, pinched into large chunks

Bread or crackers, for serving

Editor's Wine Choice
Juicy, strawberry- and watermelon-scented rosé: 2013 DeMorgenzon DMZ

A few of our favorite varieties of cherry tomatoes to grow are heirloom Sungolds, Sweet Million, and Black Cherry. At the peak of summer, cherry tomatoes are nature's candy, and to munch on a handful of them and appreciate their pops of natural sugar is a simple treat. But it can be hard to keep up with them when they all explode on the vines at once. Roasting them with some goat cheese in a great savory dip to spread on crackers is a terrific way to manage surplus cherry bombs and highlight fresh cherry tomatoes as appetizers.

1. Preheat the oven to 350°F (175°C). Lightly oil a 5- to 6-inch (12.5- to 15-cm) baking dish.

2. In a small bowl, combine 1 tablespoon of the oil with the tomatoes. Set aside.

3. In a medium bowl, mix together the ricotta, garlic, remaining 2 tablespoons oil, parsley, salt, lemon zest, and lemon juice.

4. Fold the goat cheese into the ricotta mixture.

5. In the baking dish, layer half of the cheese mixture, then add half of the tomatoes. Layer the remaining cheese mixture, then top with the remaining tomatoes. Gently press the top layer of tomatoes into the cheese mixture.

6. Bake, uncovered, until the cheese is melted and the tomatoes are evenly roasted, 25 to 40 minutes. (Cooking time will depend on the thickness of the tomato skins and the depth of the baking dish.)

7. Serve warm with bread or crackers.

For parties, this is a great dip to prep ahead.

ROASTED-CORN TABOULI

Serves **6**

- 1 cup (140 grams) uncooked bulgur
- 3 medium ears corn, husks and kernels removed
- ¼ cup (60 ml) vegetable oil
- ½ cup (30 grams) chopped fresh flat-leaf parsley
- ½ cup (40 grams) chopped fresh mint leaves
- Zest of 1 lemon
- 3 tablespoons fresh lemon juice
- 1 teaspoon kosher or sea salt
- ¼ teaspoon cayenne
- Freshly cracked black pepper

Homemade tabouli made with a mix of fresh parsley and mint leaves is such a treat, especially when we add in roasted corn. The sweet pops of corn kernels in this salad make it one of the highlights of summer. If you really love your corn, just double the amount of roasted corn in the recipe. You won't be disappointed.

1. Preheat the oven to 450°F (230°C).

2. In a saucepan, combine the bulgur with 2 cups (480 ml) water. Bring the water to a boil, then remove the pan from the heat. Cover, and allow to sit for 20 minutes, until the water has been absorbed. Set aside to cool.

3. In a bowl, combine the corn kernels with 2 tablespoons of the oil and toss to coat. Arrange the kernels in a single layer on a baking sheet and roast for 8 to 10 minutes, or until cooked through. Allow to cool.

4. In a large bowl, combine the bulgur, corn kernels, parsley, and mint. In a small bowl, combine the lemon zest, lemon juice, remaining 2 tablespoons oil, salt, cayenne, and pepper to taste.

5. Add the lemon juice mixture into the corn mixture and chill for 15 minutes before serving.

LEMON & CREAM SPAGHETTI

Serves **4 to 6**

- ½ pound (225 grams) dry spaghetti
- 2 tablespoons olive oil
- 2 tablespoons heavy cream
- ½ cup (120 ml) dry white wine
- 1 tablespoon fresh lemon zest, or more to taste
- 2 tablespoons fresh lemon juice, or more to taste
- ½ cup (50 grams) freshly grated Parmigiano Reggiano, or more to taste, plus extra for serving

Editor's Wine Choice
Zippy, citrusy Vermentino:
2013 Argiolas Costamolino

When we dine in New York, our dear friend Jennifer Perillo is our trusted guide to some of the most incredible Italian food in the city. During one dinner at a restaurant, she introduced us to the most simple yet wonderful spaghetti dishes we've ever tasted. We embarrassed ourselves by inhaling one of the dishes so fast you'd think we'd never eaten pasta before: perfectly cooked spaghetti laced with bright, floral notes of lemon and prepared in a light cream sauce. From the first to the very last bite, we marveled at how such a simple dish could be so unforgettably delicious. We've created our own version so that we can enjoy it at home. With four lemon trees in our garden, we're always prepared to indulge in this beloved pasta dish.

1. Fill a large pot with water, salt it well, and bring the water to a boil. Cook the spaghetti according to the package directions, or until al dente.

2. When the pasta is halfway cooked, begin making the sauce: In a sauté pan large enough to later hold the pasta, whisk together the oil, cream, and wine. Over medium-high heat, bring the mixture to a simmer and cook for 2 to 3 minutes, whisking occasionally.

3. Drain the pasta and add it to the sauté pan. Add the lemon zest, lemon juice, and cheese and toss well. Taste for seasoning and add a touch more lemon or cheese, if desired.

4. Serve on warm plates with additional cheese on the side.

CUCUMBER MINT QUINOA SALAD WITH SHALLOT VINAIGRETTE

Serves **4 to 6**

FOR THE SHALLOT DRESSING

- ¼ cup (60 ml) olive or grapeseed oil
- 3 large shallots, minced
- 3 medium cloves garlic, minced
- 2 teaspoons sugar
- 2 tablespoons soy sauce
- 1 teaspoon sesame oil
- ¼ teaspoon kosher or sea salt
- 1 tablespoon rice vinegar
- 1 tablespoon fresh lemon juice
- Freshly cracked black pepper

FOR THE SALAD

- 1 cup (170 grams) raw quinoa (see Note)
- 1 cup (135 grams) diced cucumber
- ½ cup (40 grams) chopped fresh mint leaves, or more to taste

We're still trying to figure out why we've never had a successful cucumber-growing season. Normally we'll get a batch of about ten cucumbers that look great, but after that, our cucumber vines fizzle into oblivion. We're still not giving up, and hopefully one year we'll have enough to satisfy our cucumber cravings. It's salads like this one that really let cucumbers shine and make us crave them even more; it's full of crunchy freshness, and the mint-quinoa combination makes it a perfect summer picnic dish to share with friends.

1. Make the shallot dressing In a saucepan, heat 2 tablespoons of the olive or grapeseed oil over medium-low heat. Add the shallots and garlic and cook until a light golden brown or until fragrant, about 2 minutes. Immediately remove the pan from the heat and add the remaining 2 tablespoons olive or grapeseed oil, the sugar, soy sauce, sesame oil, salt, vinegar, lemon juice, and pepper to taste. Stir until the sugar dissolves and all the ingredients are well combined. Set aside to marinate briefly.

2. Make the salad In a saucepan, combine the quinoa with 2 cups (480 ml) water. Bring to a simmer, cover, then reduce the heat to low and cook for 15 minutes, or until the water is fully absorbed. Place the cooled quinoa in a large bowl. Add the cucumbers and chopped mint and stir to combine.

3. Add the shallot dressing and toss well to coat. Serve immediately, or chill in the refrigerator and toss again before serving.

NOTE For a warm quinoa dish, toss the cucumbers and herbs with the quinoa while it is still warm. Prepare the dressing as instructed and toss with the warm quinoa mixture. Serve immediately.

Soy sauce
and sesame oil
change up
the usual
quinoa salad.

QUICK PICKLED SUGAR SNAP PEAS WITH MINT

Makes **1 pound (455 grams)**

- 1 **pound (455 grams) sugar snap peas or snow peas, ends trimmed**
- ½ **medium onion, sliced thin**
- ½ **cup (30 grams) chopped fresh mint**

FOR THE PICKLING BRINE

- ⅔ **cup (160 ml) distilled white vinegar**
- **Zest of 1 large lemon**
- **Juice of 1 large lemon (about 3 tablespoons)**
- 1 **tablespoon sugar**
- 1 **tablespoon kosher salt**
- 2 **teaspoons coriander seeds**
- 1 **teaspoon cumin seeds**

From Diane: I'm a pickle addict, and it's an understatement to say I can be impatient if I have to wait for a batch of fresh pickles to be ready. So I created a recipe that is quick but doesn't sacrifice flavor or texture. When I'm in a hurry to make an appetizer plate of cheese and charcuterie for a party, this pickled peas recipe is the answer. The fresh mint and lemon juice quickly season and pickle the peas to a tangy and flavorful crisp. Even without the cheese platter, these pickles are a satisfying snack, bright and full of crunch. They're also delicious stuffed in your favorite sandwich in place of regular cucumber pickles.

Depending on the size of your container, you may need to make extra pickling brine to top it off.

1. In a 2-quart (2-liter) jar, layer the peas, onion, and mint.

2. Make the pickling brine In a large bowl, combine 1 cup (240 ml) water with all the brine ingredients.

3. Pour the brine into the container with the peas, covering them completely.

4. Refrigerate for at least 2 hours before eating.

These pickles make fun Bloody Mary garnishes.

_____

POACHED EGGS IN TOMATO SAUCE

Total **30 min**
Serves **4**

3 tablespoons unsalted butter

1 small onion, minced

3 garlic cloves, minced

One 28-ounce can crushed tomatoes

1 tablespoon Worcestershire sauce

½ teaspoon sugar

¼ teaspoon cumin

¼ cup chopped parsley, plus more for garnish

Kosher salt and pepper

4 large eggs

Grilled bread, for serving

_____

Editor's Wine Choice Lively, light-bodied Beaujolais: 2012 Julien Sunier Fleurie

This simple recipe from Porter and Cu is great for brunch. With extra add-ins (kale, chickpeas, ground chicken), the dish can also be hearty enough for dinner.

1. In a large saucepan, melt the butter. Add the onion and garlic and cook over moderate heat, stirring occasionally, until softened and just starting to brown, about 8 minutes. Add the crushed tomatoes with their juices, the Worcestershire sauce, sugar and cumin and bring just to a boil. Stir in the ¼ cup of parsley and simmer over moderately low heat, stirring occasionally, until the sauce is slightly thickened, about 10 minutes. Season with salt and pepper.

2. Using the back of a spoon, make 4 depressions in the sauce. Carefully crack the eggs into the depressions, cover the pan and simmer the eggs over moderately low heat until the whites are set and the yolks are runny, about 7 minutes. Garnish with chopped parsley and serve right away, with grilled bread.

For more on Todd Porter & Diane Cu

whiteonricecouple.com

White On Rice Couple

@WhiteOnRice

THE BEEKMAN 1802 HEIRLOOM DESSERT COOKBOOK

100 Delicious Heritage Recipes from the Farm & Garden

BY **BRENT RIDGE** & **JOSH KILMER-PURCELL** & **SANDY GLUCK**

FARMSTEADERS Brent Ridge and Josh Kilmer-Purcell love heirlooms. The founders of the Beekman 1802 artisanal food and crafts line–and onetime reality TV stars–share a passion for vintage brands and antiques. In their most recent book, the couple focus on what they call "heritage" desserts, ones that pay homage to their past. A spot-on malted milk chocolate cake (page 192) is an ode to the small-town soda shops Kilmer-Purcell frequented when he was a kid in Wisconsin. Another freshly minted heirloom, pancake cake layered with maple cream frosting (page 190), was born from a surplus of batter after a pancake breakfast. Each recipe is accompanied by a blank space for notes–Ridge and Kilmer-Purcell's way of encouraging readers to make these heirlooms their own.

Published by Rodale, $32.50

PANCAKE CAKE WITH MAPLE CREAM FROSTING

Serves **6**

PANCAKES

- 1 cup all-purpose flour (spooned into cup and leveled off)
- ⅓ cup rye or whole wheat flour
- 2 tablespoons cornmeal
- ¼ cup granulated sugar
- 2 tablespoons light brown sugar
- 2 teaspoons baking powder
- ½ teaspoon salt
- 1¼ cups milk
- 2 large eggs
- 2 large egg yolks
- 2 tablespoons unsalted butter, melted, plus more for the pan
- ¾ teaspoon pure vanilla extract

FILLING

- 11 ounces cream cheese, at room temperature
- ¼ cup whole-milk Greek yogurt
- 5 tablespoons maple syrup, preferably Grade B
- 3 tablespoons confectioners' sugar, sifted

We admit that we have had cake for breakfast before. Who hasn't? But how about breakfast for dessert? This recipe came about when we accidentally made too much pancake batter on Sunday morning. It's our take on a thousand-layer cake. The pancakes can be made up to a day ahead and refrigerated. The cake can be assembled up to 2 hours ahead. Not feeling like dessert? Prepare the pancakes using only 2 tablespoons of sugar and have them for breakfast.

To make the pancakes In a large bowl, whisk together the all-purpose flour, rye flour, cornmeal, granulated and brown sugars, baking powder, and salt. In a separate bowl, whisk together the milk, whole eggs, egg yolks, butter, and vanilla.

Coat an 8-inch skillet with some melted butter and heat over medium-low heat. Pour ½ cup of the batter into the pan and cook for 1½ minutes, or until large bubbles appear on the surface of the pancake. Carefully flip the pancake over and cook for 1 minute longer, or until the underside is just cooked through. Transfer to a plate and repeat with the remaining batter to make 6 pancakes and let cool to room temperature.

To make the filling In a bowl, with an electric mixer, beat the cream cheese and yogurt until smooth. Beat in 4 tablespoons of the maple syrup and the confectioners' sugar until well combined.

To assemble the cake Spread each pancake with one-sixth of the filling (about 5 tablespoons). Place one of the pancakes on a platter and stack the remaining pancakes on top. Drizzle the remaining 1 tablespoon maple syrup over the top of the cake.

Greek yogurt
makes the
frosting tangy.

MALTED MILK CHOCOLATE CAKE

Serves **12 to 16**

Softened butter and flour for the pan

½ cup malted milk powder

1⅓ cups milk

1½ teaspoons pure vanilla extract

1¾ cups all-purpose flour (spooned into cup and leveled off)

1 cup unsweetened cocoa powder

2 teaspoons baking powder

1 teaspoon baking soda

½ teaspoon salt

8 ounces (2 sticks) unsalted butter, at room temperature

1 cup granulated sugar

1 cup packed light brown sugar

4 large eggs, at room temperature

1 cup coarsely chopped malted milk balls

Somewhere in Wisconsin, Josh developed an affinity for old-fashioned soda shops. Lime rickeys, egg creams, and root beer floats all have a special place in his heart that even a wintery cold snap can't melt. Malteds are a popular soda fountain drink, and chocolate cake is an all-time favorite dessert; here they pair up for an unexpected double malted flavor that's as sweet as lips bumping together over a straw. Malted milk powder is available in the supermarket alongside the cocoa.

Preheat the oven to 350°F. Butter a 9-by-13-inch baking pan. Line the bottom with parchment or waxed paper. Butter and flour the paper.

In a bowl, dissolve the malted milk powder in the milk. Stir in the vanilla. In a separate bowl, whisk together the flour, cocoa powder, baking powder, baking soda, and salt.

In a bowl, with an electric mixer on medium speed, beat together the butter and granulated and brown sugars until fluffy. Beat in the eggs, one at a time, beating well after each addition. With the mixer on low speed, alternately add the flour mixture and the milk mixture, beginning and ending with the flour mixture. Scrape the batter into the pan. Scatter the malted milk balls over the top.

Bake for 40 minutes, or until a wooden pick inserted in the center comes out clean with some moist crumbs attached and the sides of the cake start to pull away from the pan.

Transfer to a wire rack to cool and serve the cake from the pan.

OATMEAL CREAM PIES WITH GINGER CREAM

Makes **12 cookies**

COOKIES

- 1½ cups rolled oats
- 1 cup all-purpose flour (spooned into cup and leveled off)
- ¾ teaspoon baking powder
- ½ teaspoon baking soda
- ½ teaspoon ground cinnamon
- ¼ teaspoon freshly grated nutmeg
- ¼ teaspoon ground ginger
- ¼ teaspoon salt
- 8 tablespoons (1 stick) unsalted butter, at room temperature
- ½ cup granulated sugar
- ½ cup packed light brown sugar
- 1 large egg

FILLING

- 1 package (8 ounces) cream cheese, at room temperature
- ⅓ cup confectioners' sugar, sifted
- ¼ cup finely chopped crystallized ginger

Oatmeal cookies are Brent's favorite. These crisp, saucer-size oatmeal cookies are sandwiched with a sweet creamy filling for a takeoff on a whoopie pie.

To make the cookies Position the racks in the upper and lower thirds of the oven and preheat to 350°F. Place the oats on a baking sheet and bake on the upper rack for 10 minutes, shaking the pan once or twice to prevent burning, until lightly browned and fragrant. Remove from the oven but leave the oven on for the cookies.

Line 2 large baking sheets with parchment or waxed paper.

In a bowl, whisk together the flour, baking powder, baking soda, cinnamon, nutmeg, ginger, and salt.

In a separate bowl, with an electric mixer on medium speed, beat the butter and the granulated and brown sugars until light and fluffy. Beat in the egg. Add the flour mixture, beating until just combined. Stir in the toasted oats.

Roll 2 tablespoons of the dough into a ball, or use a #30 ice cream scoop (1 ounce) and drop the dough 2 inches apart on the baking sheets. With dampened hands, flatten each to a ½-inch thickness.

Bake for 12 minutes, switching the baking sheets from top to bottom and rotating them from front to back halfway through, or until lightly browned around the edges and set. Let cool for 5 minutes on the baking sheets, then transfer to a wire rack to cool completely.

To make the filling In a bowl, with an electric mixer, beat the cream cheese and confectioners' sugar until smooth. Beat in the ginger. Spread the mixture on 12 of the cookies and then top with the remaining 12 cookies.

TIP Toasting the oats beforehand not only makes them crisp but also brings out a delicious nutty flavor.

These cookies are also perfect for ice cream sandwiches.

CARDAMOM CAKE WITH COFFEE GLAZE

Serves **10 to 12**

CAKE

Softened butter for the pan

Fine dried bread crumbs for the pan

Cooking spray

2⅓ cups cake flour (spooned into cup and leveled off), sifted

1½ teaspoons ground cardamom

1½ teaspoons baking powder

¾ teaspoon baking soda

½ teaspoon salt

½ cup pistachios

1½ cups plus 2 tablespoons granulated sugar

8 ounces (2 sticks) unsalted butter, at room temperature

4 large eggs

1 teaspoon pure vanilla extract

1 cup sour cream

GLAZE

⅔ cup confectioners' sugar

1 teaspoon espresso powder

¼ teaspoon unsweetened cocoa powder

1 tablespoon milk, plus more if needed

Cardamom has a haunting flavor and aroma, floral yet elusive, and here it pairs with pistachio nuts for a Middle Eastern take on a coffee cake.

To make the cake Preheat the oven to 350°F. Generously butter a 10- to 12-cup Bundt pan. Dust the pan with bread crumbs. Coat with cooking spray.

In a medium bowl, whisk together the flour, cardamom, baking powder, baking soda, and salt. In a food processor, combine the pistachios and 2 tablespoons of the granulated sugar and process until finely ground.

In a bowl, with an electric mixer on medium speed, beat the butter and 1½ cups of the granulated sugar together until light and fluffy. In a small bowl, whisk together the eggs and vanilla. Very gradually add the egg mixture to the butter mixture until very light in texture. Beat in the pistachio-sugar mixture.

With the mixer on low speed, alternately beat in the flour mixture and sour cream, beginning and ending with the flour mixture.

Scrape the batter into the pan and bake for 45 to 55 minutes, or until a wooden pick inserted into the cake comes out clean with some moist crumbs attached. Let cool in the pan on a wire rack, then run a metal spatula around the center and edge of the pan and invert the cake (right side up) onto a cake plate.

To make the glaze In a small bowl, whisk together the confectioners' sugar, espresso powder, and cocoa powder. Add the milk and stir until of a drizzling consistency, adding a drop or two more of milk if needed. Drizzle over the cake.

This Bundt cake has espresso powder in the glaze.

ZUCCHINI & DILL PANCAKES

Total **40 min**
Serves **4 as a first course**

- 2 medium zucchini (about 1 pound), coarsely shredded on the large holes of a box grater
- 2 scallions, finely chopped
- 1 large egg, lightly beaten
- ½ cup all-purpose flour
- ½ teaspoon baking soda
- ⅓ cup chopped dill, plus more for garnish
- Kosher salt
- ¼ cup olive oil
- Crème fraîche or sour cream, for serving

Editor's Wine Choice Melon- and citrus-scented California Sauvignon Blanc: 2013 Honig

With a guaranteed abundance of summer squash on their farm in upstate New York, Ridge and Kilmer-Purcell are always thinking of different ways to use all of their zucchini. Here they shred it and add plenty of dill to make little pancakes. Topped with crème fraîche and paired with chutney or tomato relish, the zucchini pancakes make an elegant appetizer.

1. Pile the shredded zucchini in a colander and let stand for 10 minutes. Squeeze out as much liquid as possible, then transfer the zucchini to a large bowl. Stir in the scallions, egg, flour, baking soda, the ⅓ cup of dill and ¾ teaspoon of salt.

2. Preheat the oven to 350°F. Set a paper towel–lined baking sheet near the stove. In a large skillet, heat 2 tablespoons of the oil over moderate heat until shimmering. Working in 2 batches, add 4 scant ¼-cup mounds of batter to the skillet. Using a spatula, gently flatten each mound to a ½-inch thickness and cook, turning once, until the pancakes are golden and cooked through, about 8 minutes. Transfer the pancakes to the prepared baking sheet, season with salt and repeat with the remaining oil and batter.

3. Discard the paper towels and reheat the pancakes in the oven for about 3 minutes. Arrange the pancakes on a platter, garnish with dill and serve with crème fraîche or sour cream.

SERVE WITH Dollops of chutney or tomato relish.

For more on Brent Ridge & Josh Kilmer-Purcell
beekman1802.com
Beekman 1802 Boys
@Beekman1802Boys

ORZO WITH ZUCCHINI &
GRANA PADANO, P.202

NOTES FROM THE LARDER

A Kitchen Diary with Recipes

BY **NIGEL SLATER**

NIGEL Slater is the best kind of companion in the kitchen. The beloved British cookbook author and host of his own BBC series is clever, unpretentious and not too fussy about how to prepare his recipes. His "quickest curry ever" (page 204) is the perfect example: Quantities are rough–"a generous pound" of salmon, "fairly large" tomatoes. And timing can be inexact; the tomatoes "soften for a minute or two." Slater balances consistently delicious recipes with wiggle room for home cooks to make adjustments. For his kale with chorizo (page 203)–a fun take on the traditional cabbage-and-pork pairing–he emphasizes that his recipe isn't a rule, it's a proposal. About his direction to discard the fat from the pan: "The suggestion is just that. Leave [it] in if you wish." It's comforting advice.

Published by Ten Speed Press, $40

ORZO WITH ZUCCHINI & GRANA PADANO

Enough for **4**

Orzo: 10 ounces (300 grams)

**Pancetta, in the piece:
    5 ounces (150 grams)**

A large onion

Olive oil: 2 tablespoons

White wine: 1 cup (250 ml)

Zucchini: 4 medium

**Grana Padano or Parmesan,
    very coarsely grated:
    ½ cup (50 grams)**

Editor's Wine Choice Zesty,
peach-inflected southern
Italian white: 2012 Li Veli Fiano

**Here, the grains are held together with grated cheese. I have
suggested the mild and nutty Grana Padano for a change. Use
Parmesan if you can't track it down.**

Bring a deep pan of water to a boil, salt generously, then add the
orzo and boil for nine minutes or till it is approaching softness. It should
retain a certain bite. Drain.

Cut the pancetta into large dice. Peel and chop the onion. Fry it with
the pancetta in the olive oil in a shallow, heavy pan over moderate heat
for fifteen minutes, stirring regularly, till the onion is soft and translucent and the fat on the pancetta is pale amber.

Pour in the wine, turn up the heat slightly, then sauté till reduced
by half. Cut the zucchini lengthwise, then into thick slices, and add to
the pan. Season with salt and black pepper and continue cooking
for eight to ten minutes, until the zucchini are tender. Stir in the drained
orzo and the Grana Padano or Parmesan. The cheese should melt
slightly, bringing the whole dish together.

KALE WITH CHORIZO & ALMONDS

Enough for **2 as a light main course, 4 as a side dish**

Curly kale: 9 ounces (250 grams)

Soft cooking chorizo: 9 ounces (250 grams)

Blanched whole almonds: 4 tablespoons (50 grams)

A little peanut or sunflower oil

A clove of garlic, peeled and crushed

Good-quality cooking chorizo is not the cheapest of meats but I find a little goes a long way. When this recipe was first published in my column I was asked why I suggested discarding the oil, especially as it contains so much chorizo flavor. A good point, but I felt there was enough fat in the dish already. So the suggestion is just that. Leave the spicy, orange, liquid fat in, if you wish.

Wash the kale thoroughly—the leaves can hold grit in their curls. Put several of the leaves on top of one another and shred them coarsely, discarding the really thick ends of the stalks as you go.

Cut the chorizo into thick slices. Warm a nonstick frying pan over moderate heat, add the slices of chorizo, and fry until golden. Lift them out with a slotted spoon onto a dish lined with paper towels. Discard most of the oil that has come out of the chorizo (better still, keep it for frying potatoes) and wipe the pan clean. Add the almonds and cook for two or three minutes, till pale gold, then lift out and add to the chorizo.

Warm a little oil in the pan, add the crushed garlic and shredded greens, and cook for a couple of minutes, turning the greens over as they cook, till glossy and starting to darken in color. Return the chorizo and almonds to the pan, add a little salt, and continue cooking till all is sizzling, then transfer to hot plates.

A MILD & FRUITY CURRY OF SALMON

Enough for **4**

Salmon fillet: a generous 1 pound (500 grams), skinned

A large onion

Peanut oil: 2 tablespoons

Small, hot chiles: 2, finely chopped and seeded

Mustard seeds: half a teaspoon

Ground turmeric: half a teaspoon

Ground cumin: a teaspoon

Ground coriander: a teaspoon

Tomatoes: 6 fairly large ones

Tamarind paste: a tablespoon

Coconut milk: ¾ cup (200 ml)

Editor's Wine Choice
Cherry-rich, full-bodied rosé:
2013 Montes Cherub

Tonight I throw together the quickest curry ever. Mild, sumptuous, a cinch. Serve with rice or Indian bread that you have warmed under the broiler. Tamarind paste is available in Indian and Southeast Asian shops and in major supermarkets, usually near the fish sauce.

I serve this with a spoon, so as not to waste a drop of the gently spiced juices.

Cut the salmon into about 20 thick cubes. Peel the onion and chop it finely, then let it soften in the oil in a deep nonstick pan. When it has started to color lightly, add the chiles, mustard seeds, turmeric, cumin, and coriander and stir for a minute or so till the spices are warm and fragrant. Chop the tomatoes, add them to the pan, and leave to soften for a minute or two. Stir in the tamarind paste.

Bring to a boil, then turn down to a simmer and cook for ten minutes. Add the pieces of salmon and some salt and black pepper. Now leave to cook for ten to fifteen minutes, until the salmon is completely opaque. Pour in the coconut milk and simmer for a further four or five minutes.

Tamarind paste adds a sweet-and-sour flavor.

ROASTED-GARLIC MUSHROOM TARTS

Active **30 min**; Total **2 hr**
Makes **4 tarts**

1 small head of garlic, halved horizontally

¼ cup crème fraîche

Kosher salt and pepper

7 ounces all-butter puff pastry (half of one 14-ounce sheet), chilled

1 large egg, lightly beaten

2 tablespoons unsalted butter

½ pound large button mushrooms, quartered

1 tablespoon chopped dill, plus more for garnish

Editor's Wine Choice Toasty, green apple–scented white Burgundy: 2012 Olivier Leflaive Les Sétilles

Crisp and buttery, these individual mushroom tarts have a hidden layer of garlicky crème fraîche. Slater uses store-bought puff pastry dough, which makes the tarts easy to prepare.

1. Preheat the oven to 350°F. Wrap the garlic in a sheet of foil and roast for about 1 hour, until very soft. Let cool, then squeeze the garlic cloves out of the skins into a small bowl and mash. Stir in the crème fraîche and season with salt and pepper. Refrigerate the garlic crème fraîche until ready to use.

2. Increase the oven temperature to 400°F and line a large baking sheet with parchment paper. On a lightly floured work surface, roll out the puff pastry to a 6-by-8-inch rectangle, then cut it into four 3-by-4-inch rectangles; transfer to the prepared baking sheet. Using a paring knife, lightly score a smaller rectangle onto each piece of puff pastry, leaving a ½-inch border. Poke the smaller rectangles all over with a fork and brush the edges with the beaten egg. Top with another sheet of parchment paper and another baking sheet and bake for 10 minutes. Remove the top baking sheet and parchment paper and bake the tarts until puffed and golden, about 10 minutes longer.

3. Meanwhile, in a large skillet, melt the butter. Add the mushrooms and cook over moderately high heat, stirring occasionally, until browned and tender, about 6 minutes. Stir in the 1 tablespoon of dill and season with salt and pepper.

4. Using a spoon, gently push down the inside of each tart to form a shallow well. Spread 1 heaping tablespoonful of the garlic crème fraîche into each, then top with the sautéed mushrooms. Garnish the tarts with chopped dill and serve.

MAKE AHEAD The roasted garlic can be refrigerated for up to 1 day.

For more on Nigel Slater
nigelslater.com
 @NigelSlater

Curtis Stone at his Los Angeles home, where he often entertains. "What makes a dinner party special isn't perfectly browned scallops or a sky-high soufflé. It's you," he says.

WHAT'S FOR DINNER?

Delicious Recipes for a Busy Life

BY **CURTIS STONE**

AUTHOR, chef, new father and host of Bravo's *Top Chef Masters*, Curtis Stone approaches his fifth book with a simple premise: Everyone is busy, but home cooking is always worth the effort. So Stone organizes recipes by day of the week to help home cooks plan ahead and adds notes on smart ways to save time. For a Tuesday night, Stone recommends seared snapper with an Italian salsa verde (page 212) and offers one of his many flavor-boosting tips: Caramelize the lemons in the skillet before squeezing them into the salsa. And Stone makes sure to include recipes for which the bulk of the work can be done ahead, like his Asian crab cakes with mango chutney (page 214). They are ideal for a Monday-night family supper or a Saturday-night dinner party.

Published by Ballantine Books, $35

GRILLED FISH TACOS WITH PICO DE GALLO

Prep Time **15 min;** Cooking Time **10 min**
Serves **4**

PICO DE GALLO

- 4 ripe plum tomatoes (about 1 pound total), cut into ½-inch pieces
- 1 small white onion, finely chopped
- 2 red jalapeño peppers, seeded and finely chopped
- ¼ cup finely chopped fresh cilantro
- 3 tablespoons fresh lemon juice
- 1 teaspoon kosher salt

TACOS

- 2 tablespoons olive oil
- 1 tablespoon finely chopped fresh cilantro
- 1 garlic clove, finely chopped
- 1¼ pounds fresh mahi mahi fillet, cut into 8 pieces
- Kosher salt and freshly ground black pepper
- 2 limes, halved
- Eight 6-inch corn tortillas
- 2 cups very thinly sliced green cabbage
- ¼ cup Mexican crema or sour cream
- Fresh cilantro leaves, for garnish

Editor's Wine Choice Zippy, lime-inflected Chilean Sauvignon Blanc: 2013 Casas del Bosque

I was in Hawaii when I tasted my first fish taco. I had been surfing all morning, and I was waterlogged, sun-kissed, and seriously starving when I spotted a woman at a beachside cart tucking grilled mahi mahi into tortillas. While this recipe is simple, there are a couple of things that will ensure success. Use super fresh fish, and don't leave out the cabbage—it adds a nice crunch that accentuates the tenderness of the fish. To relive the outdoor experience, I prefer to grill these, but you can also cook the fish under a hot broiler for about the same amount of time and heat the tortillas over a gas burner.

1. To make the pico de gallo In a medium bowl, toss the tomatoes, onions, jalapeños, cilantro, lemon juice, and salt together. Set aside at room temperature.

2. To make the tacos Prepare an outdoor grill for medium-high cooking over direct heat.

3. In a wide shallow bowl, whisk the olive oil, cilantro, and garlic to blend. Lightly coat the fish with the oil mixture and season with salt and pepper. Oil the cooking grate. Add the fish and grill for 2 to 3 minutes per side, or until barely opaque when flaked in the thickest part with the tip of a small knife. Using a spatula, transfer the fish to a cutting board and let stand for 2 minutes.

4. Meanwhile, grill the limes cut side down for about 3 minutes, or until they begin to char on the bottom. Remove from the grill. Add the tortillas to the grill and cook, turning halfway through, for about 1 minute, until warmed.

5. Coarsely break or cut the fish into large flaky chunks and divide it among the tortillas. Top with the cabbage, pico de gallo, crema, and a sprinkle of cilantro leaves. Serve hot with the grilled limes.

PAN-FRIED SNAPPER WITH FENNEL & SALSA VERDE

Prep Time **10 min;** Cooking Time **20 min**
Serves **4**

SALSA VERDE

- ½ cup extra-virgin olive oil
- 3 tablespoons finely chopped scallions (white and green parts)
- 2 tablespoons chopped fresh basil
- 2 tablespoons chopped fresh flat-leaf parsley
- 1 teaspoon chopped fresh rosemary
- 2 tablespoons chopped drained nonpareil capers
- 1 tablespoon minced shallots

Finely grated zest of 1 lemon

Kosher salt and freshly ground black pepper

VEGETABLES & FISH

- 5 tablespoons olive oil
- 3 small fennel bulbs (about 1 pound total), trimmed and cut from tip to core into ¼-inch-thick slices
- 1 small yellow onion, thinly sliced
- 4 small lemons, cut in half crosswise

Four 6-ounce red snapper fillets with skin

Kosher salt and freshly ground black pepper

Editor's Wine Choice
Ripe, fragrant Spanish white:
2012 Paso a Paso Verdejo

Depending on the country, Mexico or Italy, salsa verde means different things. Both are green sauces, but Mexican cooks make theirs from tomatillos and cilantro. This Italian version is made with herbs, capers, shallots, olive oil, and lemon. When you want to put something more than a squeeze of lemon on your fish, make this truly great uncooked sauce that can also be served with chicken or pork.

1. To make the salsa verde In a medium bowl, whisk the olive oil, scallions, basil, parsley, rosemary, capers, shallots, and lemon zest together. Set aside at room temperature.

2. To cook the vegetables and fish Heat a large skillet over medium-high heat. Add 2 tablespoons of the olive oil, then lay half of the fennel and onion slices in the pan. Cook for about 3 minutes on each side, or until tender and golden brown (don't worry if the slices fall apart). Transfer to a plate and cover to keep warm. Repeat with 1 tablespoon of the remaining olive oil and the remaining fennel and onions. This time, place the lemon halves cut side down in the skillet alongside the vegetables and cook for about 1 minute, or until they begin to brown on the cut sides. Remove the lemons from the skillet and squeeze ¼ cup of juice from about 4 of the lemon halves. Stir the juice into the salsa verde. Season the salsa to taste with salt and pepper. Reserve the remaining lemons for serving.

3. Meanwhile, using a sharp knife, lightly score the skin side of each fillet. Season the fillets with salt and pepper. Heat a large nonstick skillet over medium-high heat. Add the remaining 2 tablespoons olive oil, then lay the snapper fillets skin side down in the skillet and cook for about 3 minutes, or until the skin is golden brown and crisp. Turn the fish over and cook for about 1 minute more, or until the fish is barely opaque when pierced in the thickest part with the tip of a small knife.

4. Divide the fennel mixture evenly among four dinner plates and place the fish alongside. Drizzle with the salsa verde and serve with the reserved caramelized lemons.

ASIAN CRAB CAKES WITH MANGO CHUTNEY

Prep Time **45 min;** Cooking Time **15 min**
Serves **6**

MANGO CHUTNEY

½ cup sugar

1 mango, pitted, peeled, and cut into ¼-inch dice

¼ cup unseasoned rice wine vinegar

2 tablespoons fresh lime juice

Kosher salt

CRAB CAKES

½ cup mayonnaise

1 large egg

2 tablespoons Thai or Vietnamese fish sauce

1 tablespoon peeled and minced fresh ginger

1 tablespoon minced fresh cilantro

1 teaspoon toasted sesame oil

1 to 2 teaspoons seeded and finely chopped red jalapeño

½ teaspoon kosher salt

Finely grated zest of 1 lime

¼ cup finely chopped green onions, white and green parts

1 pound jumbo lump crabmeat, picked over and well drained

1½ cups panko (Japanese bread crumbs)

6 tablespoons canola oil

4 tablespoons unsalted butter

½ English cucumber, sliced into thin rounds, and then into matchstick-size strips

Fresh cilantro sprigs, for garnish

Flaky sea salt, for garnish

Editor's Wine Choice Tropical fruit–inflected South African Chenin Blanc: 2013 Indaba

These Southeast Asian–inspired crab cakes make such a great impression and I love that I can make them ahead with just a little last-minute cooking. I like to serve them with a simple salad of avocado, red onion, and butter lettuce, tossed with lime juice and olive oil.

1. To make the chutney Heat a medium heavy saucepan over medium heat for 2 minutes. Add the sugar and cook without stirring, tilting the pan as needed so that the sugar cooks evenly, for about 5 minutes, or until it melts into an amber caramel. Do not stir or the caramel will crystallize. Remove from the heat and stir in the mango (the caramel will seize), then the rice vinegar and lime juice. Return to medium heat and stir constantly for about 5 minutes, or until the mango is translucent and the caramel is dissolved and syrupy. Transfer to a bowl and let cool. Season with salt.

2. To prepare the crab cakes In a large bowl, whisk the mayonnaise, egg, fish sauce, ginger, cilantro, sesame oil, jalapeños, salt, and lime zest together, then whisk in the green onions. Add the crabmeat and stir to coat, coarsely breaking apart the crabmeat, leaving small whole chunks in the mixture. Fold in the panko. Cover and refrigerate the crab mixture for 30 minutes so that the mixture is easier to form.

3. Using about ⅓ cup of the crab mixture for each cake, shape into twelve ¾-inch-thick crab cakes and place on a baking sheet.

4. To cook the crab cakes Preheat the oven to 200°F. Line a baking sheet with paper towels. Heat a large nonstick sauté pan over medium-high heat. Add 3 tablespoons of the oil and 2 tablespoons of the butter and heat until hot but not smoking. Working in two batches, fry 6 crab cakes for about 2 minutes on each side, or until crisp and golden, adjusting the heat as needed to brown evenly without scorching. Transfer to the baking sheet and keep warm in the oven. Wipe out the skillet with paper towels and repeat with the remaining 3 tablespoons canola oil, 2 tablespoons butter, and 6 crab cakes.

5. To serve, place 2 crab cakes on each of six plates. Spoon some of the mango chutney over and alongside the crab cakes. Top each with the cucumber and garnish with the cilantro sprigs and sea salt.

Mini versions
of these
crab cakes are
excellent as
hors d'oeuvres.

"A happy family starts with a home-cooked meal," says Stone, here with his wife, actress Lindsay Price, and their son, Hudson.

ONION BHAJI WITH LIME CRÈME FRAÎCHE

Total **35 min**
Makes **24 fritters**

LIME CRÈME FRAÎCHE

- ½ **cup crème fraîche**
- ½ **cup finely chopped cilantro**
- ½ **cup finely chopped mint**
- ½ **serrano chile, seeded and minced**
- ½ **teaspoon finely grated lime zest**
- 2 **tablespoons fresh lime juice**

Kosher salt

ONION BHAJI

- 1 **teaspoon mustard seeds**
- ¾ **teaspoon fennel seeds**
- ¼ **cup potato starch**
- ¼ **cup rice flour**
- 1½ **teaspoons chile powder**
- 1½ **teaspoons ground turmeric**
- 1½ **teaspoons finely grated garlic**
- 1½ **teaspoons finely grated peeled fresh ginger**

Kosher salt

- ½ **cup ice water**

One small red onion, halved and very thinly sliced

- 1 **tablespoon minced cilantro**

Grapeseed or vegetable oil, for frying

Editor's Wine Choice Fresh, green apple–scented Spanish sparkling wine: NV Castillo Perelada Brut Reserva Cava

For more on Curtis Stone
curtisstone.com
Curtis Stone
@curtis_stone

These onion *bhaji* (fritters) remind Stone of the ones he loves at the curry houses on East London's Brick Lane, but with one difference: "To avoid blowing out everyone's palates on their first bite," Stone says, "I toned down the spice." For an extra-cooling effect, he serves the *bhaji* with a lime-and-mint crème fraîche.

1. Make the lime crème fraîche In a medium bowl, whisk the crème fraîche with the cilantro, mint, chile and lime zest and juice; season with salt. Cover and refrigerate until chilled, about 15 minutes.

2. Meanwhile, make the onion bhaji In a small skillet, toast the mustard and fennel seeds over moderate heat, tossing, until fragrant, about 2 minutes. Transfer to a mortar and finely crush with a pestle. In a large bowl, whisk the potato starch with the rice flour, chile powder, turmeric, garlic, ginger, crushed seeds and ¾ teaspoon of salt. Whisk in the ice water to form a thin batter with some lumps remaining. Fold in the onion and cilantro.

3. In a large saucepan, heat 2 inches of oil to 365°F. Working in batches, spoon tablespoons of the batter into the hot oil and fry, turning occasionally, until golden and nearly crisp, 2 to 3 minutes. Using a slotted spoon, transfer the fritters to a paper towel–lined baking sheet and season with salt; serve right away, with the lime crème fraîche.

Michael Symon and his wife, Liz, have dinner at home most nights. Here, they prep Ohio sweet corn in their kitchen.

MICHAEL SYMON'S 5 IN 5

5 Fresh Ingredients + 5 Minutes = 120 Fantastic Dinners

BY **MICHAEL SYMON** WITH **DOUGLAS TRATTNER**

COOKING dinner in five minutes, using only five fresh ingredients and a few pantry staples? That would be a dubious proposition if it weren't coming from Michael Symon, ebullient Midwestern chef and co-host of ABC's *The Chew*. Symon's latest collection of family-friendly recipes is built around that formula, and it's a winning one because Symon uses easily accessible ingredients that deliver big flavor. He adds jalapeño to give his chicken diablo heat (page 224); white anchovies bring a briny taste to his orecchiette (page 222). And the beauty of his mac and cheese (page 220) is twofold: Aged cheddar provides extra flavor, and the dish can be made entirely on the stovetop.

Published by Clarkson Potter, $20

NO-BAKE MAC & CHEESE

Serves **4**

Kosher salt and freshly ground black pepper

1 **pound fresh rigatoni pasta**

2 **cups heavy cream**

1 **teaspoon hot sauce, or to taste**

½ **cup mascarpone (if you cannot find it, cream cheese will work in a pinch)**

1 **cup grated aged cheddar cheese**

½ **cup finely chopped fresh chives**

Editor's Wine Choice
Concentrated, dark-berried
Dolcetto: 2012 Anna
Maria Abbona Sorí dij But

This is a no-bake macaroni and cheese dish that still delivers all the rich and creamy goodness of more complicated recipes in a fraction of the time. I can't understand why people still make the boxed stuff when you can make it from scratch in the same amount of time. Feel free to try using other cheeses, too. This version does sacrifice the crusty, breaded topping of baked casseroles, but it's ready to enjoy in a flash and just as comforting. (And if you really miss that topping, see the note at the end.)

1. In a very large pot, bring 5 quarts water and 3 tablespoons salt to a boil. Add the pasta and cook until just al dente, about 1 minute less than the package directions. Occasionally give the pasta a stir so it doesn't stick together. Drain.

2. Meanwhile, put a 2-quart saucepan or Dutch oven over medium heat. Add the cream, hot sauce, 1 teaspoon salt, and pepper to taste and bring to a simmer. Cook until the cream has reduced by one-third, about 3 minutes. Add the mascarpone and cheddar, whisking to incorporate them into the cream.

3. When the cheeses are fully melted and blended into the sauce, add the cooked pasta and chives, stirring them into the sauce. Serve immediately.

NOTE To add a crunchy topping, spread a layer of panko or plain dry bread crumbs on top and put under a hot broiler until golden brown, about 1 minute.

ORECCHIETTE WITH WHITE ANCHOVIES & MINT

Serves **4**

Kosher salt

1 **pound fresh orecchiette pasta**

6 **tablespoons olive oil**

4 **ounces white anchovies, minced**

½ **tablespoon crushed red pepper flakes**

¾ **cup torn fresh mint leaves**

½ **cup freshly grated Parmesan cheese**

3 **tablespoons unsalted butter**

Editor's Wine Choice Minerally, lemony Italian white: 2012 Fontezoppa Verdicchio di Matelica

While on vacation in Italy with family and friends, I was planning to cook a fancy pasta dish using fresh-caught sea urchin. But when we went to the market, there was no sea urchin in sight. So I quickly improvised, grabbing some briny, beautiful white anchovies instead. What started out as a huge disappointment ended up being one of our favorite pasta dishes on the trip—and made birthday girl [actress] Stephanie March pretty happy, too.

1. In a very large pot, bring 5 quarts water and 3 tablespoons salt to a boil. Add the pasta and cook until just al dente, about 1 minute less than the package directions. Occasionally give the pasta a stir so it doesn't stick together. Scoop out and reserve 1 cup of the pasta water before draining the pasta.

2. Meanwhile, put a large skillet over low heat. Add the olive oil and then the anchovies and red pepper flakes. Cook, stirring occasionally, for 4 minutes.

3. Increase the heat to medium-high and add the reserved pasta water, stirring vigorously to blend the mixture. Add the cooked pasta to the pan, stirring it into the sauce.

4. Remove from the heat and stir in the mint, Parmesan, and butter. Serve immediately.

Seafood
lovers will
enjoy the
big anchovy
flavor here.

CHICKEN DIABLO

Serves **6**

¼ cup olive oil

Six 4-ounce boneless, skin-on chicken thighs, pounded to a ¼-inch thickness

Kosher salt and freshly ground black pepper

2 garlic cloves, sliced

1 red bell pepper, thinly sliced

1 jalapeño, sliced into rings

One 14-ounce can San Marzano tomatoes with juices

2 tablespoons capers, rinsed and drained

½ cup roughly chopped fresh flat-leaf parsley leaves

Editor's Wine Choice Robustly fruity, raspberry-rich rosé: 2012 Couly-Dutheil Chinon Rosé

Chicken Diablo—aka the devil's chicken—gets its name from its demonic heat level. Depending on the spiciness of the jalapeño pepper, this dish can range anywhere from mild to medium. But if you like things super-spicy, like my stepson, Kyle, go ahead and add another jalapeño or, if you're really brave, a habanero.

1. Put a Dutch oven over medium-high heat.

2. Add the olive oil to the preheated pan. Season both sides of the chicken with salt and pepper. Put the chicken skin-side down in the pan and cook until golden brown, about 2 minutes. Flip the chicken and cook for another 30 seconds. Add the garlic, bell pepper, jalapeño, and a pinch of salt, and cook for another 30 seconds.

3. Add ½ cup water and deglaze the pan, scraping with a wooden spoon to get the browned bits on the bottom of the pan. Cook until the liquid is reduced by half, another minute. Add the tomatoes with juices and capers, cover the pan, and cook for 2 minutes.

4. Remove the pan from the heat and stir in the parsley. Taste and adjust the seasoning, adding salt and pepper as needed. Serve immediately.

The spicy, vibrant sauce is also delicious tossed with pasta.

"Cooking doesn't have to be
intimidating or time-consuming
or expensive to be delicious."
–*Michael Symon*

QUICK PAD THAI

Active **15 min**; Total **35 min**
Serves **2**

7 ounces pad Thai rice noodles

2½ tablespoons Asian fish sauce

2½ tablespoons tamarind
concentrate (see Note)

2 tablespoons packed light brown
sugar

1½ tablespoons fresh lime juice

¾ teaspoon crushed red pepper

3 tablespoons vegetable oil

1 shallot, thinly sliced

2 garlic cloves, thinly sliced

1 large egg, lightly beaten

1 cup mung bean sprouts, plus
more for garnish

½ cup packed cilantro, chopped,
plus more for garnish

2 tablespoons roasted peanuts,
chopped

Lime wedges, for serving

Editor's Wine Choice Mineral-
driven northern Italian Pinot
Grigio: 2013 Cantina Tramin

"Pad Thai is my stepson, Kyle's, favorite food, but it's a dish that can intimidate even a professional chef," Symon says. His speedy version here is pared down yet still flavorful.

1. In a large bowl, cover the rice noodles with warm water and soak until pliable, about 30 minutes. Transfer to a colander and drain, shaking and tossing the noodles once or twice.

2. Meanwhile, in a small bowl, whisk the fish sauce with the tamarind concentrate, sugar, lime juice and crushed red pepper.

3. Heat a wok or large nonstick skillet over high heat until very hot, about 5 minutes. Add the oil and swirl to coat. Add the shallot and garlic and cook, stirring occasionally, until lightly browned, about 30 seconds. Add the noodles and stir-fry until coated with oil and beginning to soften, about 1 minute. Add the fish sauce mixture and stir-fry until the noodles are tender and heated through, 1 to 2 minutes. Scrape the noodles to one side of the pan, add the egg and cook, stirring occasionally, until nearly set, about 30 seconds. Add the 1 cup of bean sprouts, ½ cup of cilantro and the peanuts and stir-fry, keeping the eggs relatively intact, until just combined. Transfer the pad Thai to plates, garnish with bean sprouts and cilantro and serve with lime wedges.

NOTE Tamarind concentrate, also known as tamarind paste, is available at Asian markets and specialty stores.

**For more on
Michael Symon**
michael d symon
@chefsymon

HAM & GRUYÈRE
BREAD PUDDING, P.230

ONE GOOD DISH

BY **DAVID TANIS**

HOMEMADE condiments, recipes made with bread, foods to be eaten with a spoon– these are three of the chapters in David Tanis's charming, idiosyncratic, deeply personal new cookbook. After writing other books focused on three-course menus, the *New York Times* columnist and veteran of Berkeley's famed Chez Panisse now offers recipes organized to reflect how he actually eats at home, as driven by his cravings. Tanis includes finger food like cucumber spears with dill (page 231) as well as heartier dishes like a fish stew infused with lemongrass and coconut (page 234), but he isn't concerned with when or how they should be served (he doesn't have a "traditional time-of-day-for-a-certain-type-of-food mentality," he says). His emphasis is on taste, and taste only.

Published by Artisan, $26

HAM & GRUYÈRE BREAD PUDDING

Serves **4**

4 tablespoons butter, softened

1 day-old French baguette, cut into ¼-inch slices

¼ pound good-quality smoked ham, diced

6 ounces Gruyère cheese, grated

3 large eggs

2½ cups half-and-half

Salt and pepper

Grated nutmeg

6 scallions, finely slivered

Editor's Wine Choice
Strawberry-scented sparkling rosé: NV Gruet Brut Rosé

A traditional bread-and-butter pudding made with milk, egg, sugar, and spice is for some the ultimate use of an old loaf. Like French toast, it is a frugal way to make a delicious dessert. I usually prefer a savory version with ham and cheese. It's sort of like a quiche, but easier. Adding briefly cooked spinach or chard makes a lovely green version, or sprinkle in a handful of freshly chopped herbs along with the scallions.

Heat the oven to 375°F. Lightly butter a shallow 2-quart rectangular baking dish. Spread the remaining butter thinly on the slices of baguette. Line the baking dish with half the baguette slices, butter side down. Arrange the ham and half the cheese over the bread. Top with the remaining baguette slices, butter side up, and sprinkle with the remaining cheese.

Beat together the eggs and half-and-half, adding ½ teaspoon salt and pepper to taste. Grate in a little nutmeg, add the scallions, and whisk again. Pour the mixture into the baking dish, pushing down to submerge the bread if necessary.

Bake for about 45 minutes, until the custard is set but still a bit wiggly and the top is nicely browned.

CUCUMBER SPEARS WITH DILL

Serves **4 to 6**

1½ pounds small cucumbers, such as kirbys or Persians

Salt and pepper

3 garlic cloves, very thinly sliced

½ teaspoon red pepper flakes

½ teaspoon thyme leaves

2 tablespoons white wine vinegar

1 tablespoon chopped dill, tarragon, or parsley

Juice of 1 lime

I discovered the method for these salady spears quite accidentally one day when I was preparing traditional fermented dill pickles. I happened to nibble on a cucumber spear only an hour after the seasoning went on. To my surprise, it already tasted really good in its not-quite-pickled state. Now if I want something pickle-like in a hurry, I make these. It's simple: just cucumbers, garlic, salt, red pepper flakes, vinegar (sometimes a bit of lime juice too), and herbs.

These cucumbers are crisp and neither too salty nor too acidic. Good for a snack, or on a relish plate, they're really a step up from "crudités." Make a batch, eat them an hour later or the next day.

Peel the cucumbers and cut them into spears. Put them in a porcelain, glass, or stainless steel bowl and season generously with salt and pepper. Add the garlic, red pepper flakes, thyme, and vinegar and toss well. Let marinate for at least an hour, chilled.

Just before serving, add the chopped dill and lime juice and toss.

COLD CHINESE CHICKEN

Serves **4 to 6**

6 large bone-in chicken thighs (about 2 pounds)

Salt and pepper

A 2-inch piece of ginger, peeled and thickly sliced

4 garlic cloves, sliced

3 star anise

4 scallions, 2 trimmed and left whole, 2 slivered

3 tablespoons chopped cilantro

1 jalapeño, thinly sliced (optional)

2 tablespoons toasted sesame oil

Lime wedges

Editor's Wine Choice Lime-inflected, dry Australian Riesling: 2013 Yalumba Y Series

I love cold chicken: cold roast chicken, cold fried chicken, perhaps especially cold boiled chicken. It is a most welcome snack on a hot day.

This is an easy dish, put together in minutes and abandoned for an hour over a low flame. Try to cook it a day ahead and let its flavors deepen with a night in the fridge. To serve, sprinkle the ice-cold jellied chicken with sesame oil and scallions, then give it a squeeze of lime. If you want something extra, add cucumber, avocado, and crisp lettuce leaves. Or take off the skin, shred the chicken, and have it with cold noodles.

Buy the best chicken you can, even if it costs more (it will). Factory chickens always taste flabby, no matter what you do. Choose a free-range bird for the flavor, the food politics, and, not least, the meaty thighs.

Season the chicken thighs generously with salt and pepper. Put them in a pot and barely cover with cold water. Add the ginger, garlic, star anise, and the 2 whole scallions, bring to a gentle boil, and skim any rising foam. Turn the heat to very low, cover, and cook at a bare simmer for 1 hour.

Transfer the thighs to a bowl to cool. Skim the fat from the surface of the cooking liquid. Over high heat, reduce the liquid by half, about 10 minutes. Strain the broth over the thighs, let cool, then cover and refrigerate for at least several hours, or overnight.

To serve, arrange the chicken on a platter, leaving some of the jellied broth clinging to it. Lightly sprinkle with salt and pepper. Top with the slivered scallions, cilantro, and, if you like, jalapeño slices. Drizzle with the sesame oil and surround with lime wedges to serve.

VERY GREEN FISH STEW

Serves **4**

FOR THE GREEN SAUCE
(MAKES ABOUT 1 CUP)

- 1 **cup cilantro leaves and tender stems (about 2 ounces)**
- 1 **cup basil leaves (about 2 ounces)**
- ¼ **cup mint leaves (about ½ ounce)**
- A 2-inch piece of fresh ginger, **peeled and thickly sliced**
- 2 **garlic cloves**
- 2 **small serrano or fresh Thai chiles, chopped**
- ½ **cup grated unsweetened coconut (fresh, dried, or frozen)**
- A 4-inch length of lemongrass, **tender center only, sliced ¼ inch thick**
- 2 **teaspoons fish sauce**
- 2 **teaspoons brown sugar**
- ½ **teaspoon salt**
- Ice water (optional)

- 1½ **pounds firm white-fleshed fish fillet, cut into 1-inch chunks**
- Salt and pepper
- 2 **tablespoons coconut or vegetable oil**
- 2 **cups chicken broth, vegetable broth, or water**
- 3 or 4 scallions, thinly sliced
- Lime wedges

Editor's Wine Choice Tangy, herbal New Zealand Sauvignon Blanc: 2013 Mt. Beautiful

I wanted this simple fish stew to be especially herbaceous, so I used lots of cilantro, basil, and mint, along with the pungent flavors of lemongrass, chiles, and ginger. For tropical sweetness, I added both coconut and coconut oil. The resulting broth is bright, spicy, satisfying, and most definitely green. The green sauce could also be stirred into a pot of steamed clams or mussels.

To make the green sauce, put the cilantro, basil, mint, ginger, garlic, chiles, coconut, lemongrass, fish sauce, sugar, and salt in a blender or food processor. Quickly process to make a smooth, thick puree, adding a little ice water if necessary. Taste and adjust the seasoning; it should be quite spicy.

Season the fish chunks lightly with salt and pepper. Heat the oil in a wide deep pan over medium heat. Add the fish and fry lightly for 1 minute on one side. Flip the fish and raise the heat to medium-high. Add the broth and half of the green sauce, then put on the lid and cook for 2 minutes, or just until the fish is opaque throughout. Gently stir in the remaining green sauce. Taste the broth and adjust the salt if necessary. Ladle the stew into bowls, sprinkle with the scallions, and serve with lime wedges.

For more on David Tanis
davidtanis.com
David Tanis
@DavidTanisCooks

A quick herb
puree forms
the base
of this stew.

Amy Thielen at home in Minnesota; for years she cooked on a 1940s-era stove.

THE NEW MIDWESTERN TABLE

200 Heartland Recipes

BY **AMY THIELEN**

AMY Thielen, host of Food Network's *Heartland Table*, grew up in rural northern Minnesota on foraged mushrooms, home-smoked sausage and potluck buffets. After cooking at a few highly regarded New York City restaurants, she returned to Minnesota and reacquainted herself with the food of her childhood, adding the creativity she'd explored in Manhattan. Her first cookbook is full of brilliant twists on regional standards, like fire-and-iceberg salad (page 242)—with cayenne pepper, it's a spicy riff on iceberg with French dressing—and slow-cooked beef pot roast made modern with pistachio salt (page 238). Other recipes, like tender milk-cooked cabbage (page 244), are pulled straight from family traditions.

Published by Clarkson Potter, $35

CLASSIC BEEF POT ROAST WITH PISTACHIO SALT

Serves **8**

One 4-pound beef chuck roast, the more marbled the better

Fine sea salt and freshly ground black pepper

1 tablespoon canola oil

2 tablespoons salted butter

3 stalks celery, cut into thirds

3 large carrots, quartered

2 medium turnips, quartered

¾ cup dry red wine

2 cups beef stock, low-sodium store-bought or homemade

2 large Vidalia onions, cut into eighths

11 cloves garlic: 10 whole, 1 minced (see Note on page 240)

4 dried bay leaves

1 tablespoon minced fresh rosemary

1 tablespoon minced fresh thyme

1 cup cherry tomatoes

¼ cup shelled salted pistachios, chopped

¼ cup chopped fresh parsley

Editor's Wine Choice
Peppery, concentrated Sicilian red: 2012 Valle dell'Acate Case Ibidini Nero d'Avola

For years I cooked on a 1940s-era Roper stove, a stocky thing with four widely spaced burners and husky, white enameled shoulders.

For all its bulk, the stove had a tiny ovenbox, and on the open door was printed a chart titled "Roper Scientific Cooking Chart," whose recommendations were a bit at odds with today's kitchen wisdom. At the far left of the spectrum, under "Low Temperature Cookery, 275°F," were the words "beef roast, pork roast, veal and ham." Lately, possibly in reaction to our accelerated lifestyles, most pot-roasted beef recipes call for an oven temperature of 325°F. And yet from my professional cooking days I remember always setting the oven temperature for such covered-dish braises lower, to 285°F, a magic number that cooks the meat slowly without causing the liquid to boil and the meat to toughen.

So in equal emulation of both early-twentieth-century farm women and twenty-first-century professional chefs, I braise my pot roast at 285°F for almost five hours, during which time it obediently sinks into its own juices. At this temperature the pot roast takes about an hour longer than a higher-temperature braise, but the cooking time is largely hands-off, and it gives me plenty of time to stir together a quick pistachio salt topping. Modeled on the traditional Italian *gremolata*, it functions here as a finishing salt for the meat.

Season the roast liberally with salt and pepper. Heat your largest high-sided skillet over high heat, add the oil, and then add the roast. Sear it quickly until dark brown on all sides, about 8 minutes. Set the roast aside, pour off and discard the excess fat from the skillet, and let the skillet cool a bit. Then add the butter, celery, carrots, turnips, ½ teaspoon salt, and ¾ teaspoon pepper. Cook over medium heat, tossing, until the vegetables begin to soften at the edges, about 5 minutes. Transfer them to a wide bowl and reserve.

Preheat the oven to 300°F.

Add the wine to the skillet, bring to a boil, and cook until slightly reduced, about 3 minutes. Add the beef stock, and bring to a simmer.

continued on page 240

CLASSIC BEEF POT ROAST WITH PISTACHIO SALT *continued*

Arrange the onions in the bottom of a large covered roasting pan and set the beef on top of them. Scatter the whole garlic cloves, bay leaves, rosemary, and thyme over and around the roast. Pour the beef stock mixture over the meat and cover the pan tightly. Bake for 1 hour.

Reduce the oven temperature to 285°F, and continue to braise for 2 hours.

Uncover the pan, skim off the fat around the edges with a small ladle, and discard it. With two large forks, carefully turn the meat over and ladle some juice over the top. Add the reserved sautéed vegetables, arranging them around the perimeter of the meat. Cover the pan and braise for 1 more hour.

Skim the fat again with a small ladle, baste the top of the meat again, and then scatter the cherry tomatoes across the top, some dropping onto the meat, some onto the vegetables. Don't stir again. Braise, uncovered this time to allow the tomatoes to split and shrink and the top of the meat to brown, until the meat feels extremely tender at the touch of a fork, 30 minutes to 1 hour. Discard the bay leaves.

For the pistachio salt, combine the pistachios, parsley, minced garlic, and ¼ teaspoon each of salt and pepper in a small bowl.

Before serving, dust the pistachio salt evenly over the roast (reserve any extra for passing at the table). Serve the pot roast right from the pan, pulling apart the meat with two forks for most of it, and gently carving the marbled top end of the chuck into thick slices.

NOTE It's easy to peel a large quantity of garlic if you use the method I learned from New York's finest prep cooks: Split apart the garlic cloves, discarding all excess papery skin, and soak them in a bowl of water for at least 20 minutes. Then peel the garlic with a small knife (a small serrated one works really well). The cloves will pop right out of their skins.

Thielen's husband, Aaron, and son, Hank, relax in the backyard of their Northwoods Minnesota cabin, where the couple used to live without electricity or running water.

FIRE & ICEBERG SALAD

Serves **6 to 8**

½ **clove garlic, finely grated**

1 **teaspoon tomato paste**

1 **teaspoon sweet paprika**

½ **teaspoon smoked paprika**

1 **tablespoon honey**

2 **tablespoons red or white wine vinegar**

1 **tablespoon fresh lemon juice**

7 **tablespoons extra-virgin olive oil**

⅛ **teaspoon cayenne pepper, or to taste**

Fine sea salt and freshly ground black pepper

½ **cup (2 ounces) walnut halves or pieces**

1 **tablespoon salted butter**

½ **large head (1 pound) iceberg lettuce, outer leaves removed**

1 **small head (7 ounces) radicchio**

1 **light green celery heart, thinly sliced**

4 **ounces blue cheese, crumbled**

At my child's preschool they sometimes serve miniature piles of torn iceberg lettuce tossed with French dressing. I can understand why: The crunch is fun and the dressing candy-sweet.

When made at home, where you can control the sugar and add some heat and smoked paprika, French dressing is a more interesting concoction. I like it spicy, because I find that a little chile fire goes a long way toward igniting the cold crisp heart of the iceberg. Ripped radicchio—raging pink—adds color and maturity.

For the dressing, combine the garlic, tomato paste, both paprikas, honey, vinegar, and lemon juice in a small bowl, and stir to combine. Whisk in 6 tablespoons of the olive oil. Season with the cayenne, ¼ teaspoon salt, and ⅛ teaspoon pepper. Pour the dressing into a small pitcher for serving at the table.

To toast the walnuts, combine them with the remaining 1 tablespoon olive oil and the tablespoon of butter in a small skillet set over medium-low heat. Season with salt and pepper. Cook, tossing regularly, until the walnuts are fragrant and have turned golden brown, about 5 minutes. Let the nuts cool.

Tear the iceberg lettuce and the radicchio into bite-size pieces, and combine in a large salad bowl. Add the celery and the walnuts (cooking fat and all), and toss to combine. Sprinkle the blue cheese over the top and serve immediately, passing the dressing alongside.

NOTE For perfect crispiness, let each person drizzle the dressing over his or her own salad. Tossing the iceberg with the dressing before it reaches the table causes the lettuce to wilt.

For extra fire, add your favorite hot sauce to the dressing.

MILK CABBAGE

Serves **6**

- 3 tablespoons salted butter
- 2 cloves garlic, minced
- 1 very small sprig fresh rosemary
- 8 cups (packed) shredded cabbage
- ¾ teaspoon salt
- ½ teaspoon freshly ground black pepper
- ¾ cup whole milk
- ½ cup walnuts, toasted (see Cold-Toasting Nuts) and roughly chopped

I was buying raspberry bushes at Brenda Bozovsky's nursery, a few miles east of my place, when the talk rolled around to cabbage. She must have had fifty of them in her garden, their bald heads exposed to the sun. Originally from North Dakota, Brenda's mother gave a lot of their garden vegetables a bath in milk, most notably the green ones: the peas, the beans, and "oh, the milk cabbage. . . , " she burst out. "That is just the best!"

A farmhouse tradition modernized with a little rosemary and a few toasted walnuts, this is excellent served next to steamed rice, mashed potatoes, or any kind of starch capable of sopping up the creamy cruciferous juice.

Shave the cabbage as you would for coleslaw—about the width of two nickels. The cooking goes quickly, so be sure to stand nearby so you can pull the pan from the heat the second the cabbage softens.

Heat the butter in a large saucepan over medium heat, and add the garlic. Cook until fragrant, about 1 minute. Add the rosemary, cabbage, salt, and pepper and stir to mix. Pour in the milk, raise the heat slightly, and bring the milk to a simmer. Then reduce the heat to medium, cover the pan, and cook, stirring once, until the cabbage is just tender—not crunchy any longer but not mushy, either—4 to 7 minutes. Discard the rosemary sprig.

Transfer the cabbage to a shallow serving bowl (I like a shallow oval dish for this one), top it with the toasted walnuts, and serve.

COLD-TOASTING NUTS When I need to toast nuts in the oven (skin-on hazelnuts, for instance, or whole almonds) but don't need the oven for baking anything else, I give the nuts a cold start, so as not to waste time or propane: I put the nuts in the oven, turn it to 350°F, and then set a timer. Every oven will heat at a different rate, so this is not an exact science, but in my oven pecans toast in 10 minutes, almonds in 15, walnuts in 20, and hazelnuts in 25 minutes. This method is especially valuable during the hot days of summer, when you want to keep the heat-throwing-appliance usage to a minimum.

APPLE CIDER SCONE CAKE

Active **20 min;** Total **1 hr**
Serves **8**

- 5 cups good-quality apple cider
- 2⅓ cups all-purpose flour
- 1½ teaspoons baking soda
- ½ teaspoon baking powder
- ½ teaspoon fine sea salt
- 1½ sticks unsalted butter, melted and cooled
- ½ cup granulated sugar
- 2 large eggs
- ½ cup sour cream
- ¾ cup packed dark brown sugar
- ¾ cup heavy cream
- 1½ tablespoons whiskey
- Unsweetened whipped cream, for serving

"Boiling down apple cider to make a tangy, sweet syrup is an old rural American trick worth bringing back," Thielen says. She bakes dollops of thick, buttery scone batter on top of cider syrup, resulting in a fluffy, biscuit-like cake with a sticky cider caramel base. **"Definitely serve this one warm, right from the baking dish,"** Thielen advises.

1. Preheat the oven to 350°F. In a large skillet, boil the apple cider over moderately high heat until reduced to 2 cups, about 25 minutes.

2. Meanwhile, in a medium bowl, whisk the flour with the baking soda, baking powder and salt. In a standing mixer fitted with the whisk attachment, beat the butter with the granulated sugar at high speed until pale yellow, about 2 minutes. At medium speed, beat in the eggs one at a time until very thick, about 2 minutes. Beat in the sour cream. Using a rubber spatula, fold in the dry ingredients until just combined; the batter will be slightly dry and resemble cookie dough.

3. Whisk the brown sugar, cream and whiskey into the reduced apple cider in the skillet, then pour the cider syrup into a 9-by-13-inch glass or ceramic baking dish. Dollop eight ⅓-cup mounds of batter evenly over the cider syrup and bake for about 20 to 25 minutes, until the top of the cake is golden brown and the syrup is bubbling. Let stand for 10 minutes before serving with whipped cream.

For more on Amy Thielen
amythielen.com
Amy Thielen
@amyrosethielen

PAPPA AL POMODORO
WITH CHICKPEAS, P.248

COLLARDS & CARBONARA

Southern Cooking, Italian Roots

BY **ANDREW TICER** & **MICHAEL HUDMAN**
WITH **NICHOLAS TALARICO**

ANDREW Ticer and Michael Hudman grew up surrounded by big Italian families, and together they run two fantastic restaurants in Memphis that embrace the cooking of both the American South and Italy. They specialize in elegant and sometimes surprising comfort food: The *pappa al pomodoro* (pictured at left), a hearty bread and tomato soup, is true to its Tuscan peasant roots, but Ticer and Hudman serve it with lemony, garlicky chickpea crostini for an untraditional touch. Their romaine salad (page 252) is a play on a classic Caesar, only instead of croutons, they add their favorite element of Southern fried chicken–the crispy skin. Using the combined flavors of their Italian-Southern pantry, Ticer and Hudman prove the two cuisines to be wonderfully in sync.

Published by Olive Press, $35

PAPPA AL POMODORO WITH CHICKPEAS

Makes **6 servings**

Olive oil

1 **yellow onion and ½ red onion, diced**

1 **fennel bulb, diced**

2 **stalks celery, diced**

1 **cup (8 fluid ounces/250 ml) dry white wine**

6 **tomatoes, diced**

8 **cups (64 fluid ounces/2 liters) Chicken Stock (recipe follows)**

One 3-ounce (90-gram) piece Parmigiano-Reggiano cheese rind

One 1-pound (500-gram) day-old coarse country bread, cut into small cubes

1 **sprig fresh basil**

Kosher salt and freshly ground pepper

FOR THE CHICKPEA CROSTINI

6 **pieces coarse country bread, each ½ inch (12 mm) thick**

2 **cups (12 ounces/370 grams) drained cooked chickpeas**

1 **teaspoon Roasted Garlic (page 254)**

Finely grated zest of 1½ lemons

Juice of ½ lemon

¼ **cup (2 fluid ounces/60 ml) extra-virgin olive oil**

Kosher salt and freshly ground pepper

Canola oil for deep-frying

1 **sprig fresh rosemary**

2 **sprigs fresh flat-leaf parsley**

This is our interpretation of *pappa al pomodoro*, a hearty Tuscan soup traditionally made with day-old bread. It's a peasant dish, using inexpensive staples that home cooks generally have on hand. The bread is added to give it substance. We like the depth of flavor that the bread adds, too, so we use a lot of it, plus we like to serve the soup with an extra piece of toasted bread spread with a purée of chickpeas, olive oil, garlic, and lemon. We top the purée with fried herbs and garbanzo beans, and finish it off with freshly grated lemon zest. —*Michael*

In a soup pot, warm a glug (about 1 tablespoon) of olive oil over medium-high heat. Add the yellow and red onions and sauté until translucent, about 5 minutes. Add the fennel and sauté briefly, then add the celery and sauté until the vegetables are soft, about 10 minutes. Stir in the wine and cook until nearly evaporated. Add the tomatoes, stock, cheese rind, three-fourths of the bread cubes, and the basil and bring to a boil. Reduce the heat to low and simmer until the liquid is reduced by about one-third, about 20 minutes. Taste and season with salt and pepper.

Meanwhile, preheat the oven to 500°F (260°C). Spread the remaining bread cubes on a baking sheet and toast in the oven until golden brown, about 5 minutes. Remove from the oven and set aside.

To make the crostini, arrange the bread slices on a baking sheet and toast in the oven until golden brown, about 5 minutes. Set aside.

In a food processor, combine 1 cup (6 ounces/185 grams) of the chickpeas, the roasted garlic, two-thirds of the lemon zest, and the lemon juice and pulse until the chickpeas are finely chopped. With the machine running, slowly add the olive oil until the mixture is smooth. Season to taste with salt and pepper.

Pour canola oil into a deep-fryer to the fill line or to a depth of 2 inches (5 cm) into a tall-sided saucepan. Heat the oil to 350°F (180°C) on a deep-frying thermometer. Add the remaining 1 cup chickpeas, the rosemary, and the parsley to the hot oil and fry until crisp, about 20 seconds. Remove the chickpeas and herbs from the oil and drain on paper towels. Put the fried chickpeas and herbs in a bowl and toss with the remaining lemon zest and salt and pepper to taste.

To serve, spread the chickpea purée on the toasted bread slices and top with the fried chickpea mixture. Ladle the soup into warmed bowls. Drop the toasted bread cubes into the soup, dividing them evenly among the bowls. Accompany each bowl with a chickpea crostini.

Chicken Stock

Preheat the oven to 500°F (260°C). Spread the chicken bones on a large rimmed baking sheet and roast until golden brown, 15 to 20 minutes.

In a stockpot, combine the roasted bones, onions, carrot, celery, garlic, bay leaves, thyme, parsley, peppercorns, and cheese rind. Add water to cover by 2 inches (5 cm) and bring to a boil over high heat. Reduce the heat to low and simmer, uncovered, until the stock is full flavored and the liquid has reduced by one-third, about 4 hours. While the stock simmers, from time to time, use a large metal spoon to skim off the grayish foam that rises to the surface.

Strain the stock through a fine-mesh sieve and discard the solids. If using right away, let the stock stand for a few minutes, then skim off the fat from the surface before using. Or, to store the stock, let cool completely, transfer to an airtight container, and refrigerate for up to 3 days or freeze for up to 3 months. Scrape off the solidified fat from the surface of the stock before using.

Makes **about 3 quarts (3 liters)**

- 5 **pounds (2.5 kg) chicken bones**
- 2 **yellow onions, chopped**
- 1 **carrot, chopped**
- 1 **stalk celery, chopped**
- 1 **head garlic, cut in half crosswise**
- 3 **dried bay leaves**
- 1 **bunch fresh thyme**
- 1 **bunch fresh flat-leaf parsley**
- 1 **tablespoon peppercorns**
- 1 **Parmigiano-Reggiano cheese rind**

Kosher salt

CHICKEN CACCIATORE

Makes **6 servings**

8 chicken drumsticks

8 chicken thighs

Kosher salt and freshly ground pepper

¼ cup (2 fluid ounces/60 ml) olive oil

1 bunch celery, stalks diced and leaves reserved

2 carrots, sliced

1 fennel bulb, sliced

1 yellow onion, sliced

2 tablespoons Roasted Garlic (page 254)

1 tablespoon tomato paste

1 cup (8 fluid ounces/250 ml) dry white wine

1 can (28 ounces/875 grams) crushed tomatoes

1 bunch fresh thyme

1 bunch fresh flat-leaf parsley

4 cups (32 fluid ounces/1 liter) Chicken Stock (page 249)

Juice of 1 lemon

Editor's Wine Choice
Medium-bodied Sangiovese:
2011 Coltibuono Cetamura
Chianti Classico

This hunter-style chicken is a soul-satisfying dish. Both of our grandmothers made a version, and we have long argued over whose was better. We once cooked it for our staff meal, and it went over so well, and we had so much left over, that we had to do something else with it. We picked the meat off the bone and made a sauce for gnocchi, which is now the only way Andy likes to eat it. It's also good over polenta, white beans, or pasta. That's why you should always save leftovers! —*Michael*

Preheat the oven to 400°F (200°C).

Season the chicken all over with salt and pepper. Warm a Dutch oven over medium-high heat and add the olive oil. When the oil is hot, add the chicken pieces and cook, turning once, until well browned on both sides, about 4 minutes per side. Transfer the chicken to a plate. Add the celery, carrots, fennel, onion, and roasted garlic to the Dutch oven and cook over medium-high heat until the vegetables start to caramelize, about 7 minutes, stirring once halfway through. Add the tomato paste and sauté for 5 minutes. Add the wine and stir to scrape up the brown bits on the pan bottom.

Add the tomatoes, thyme, parsley, and stock to the pot and bring the liquid to a simmer. Return the chicken to the pot, cover, and put the pot in the oven. Bake until the chicken meat begins to pull away from the bone, 45 to 60 minutes.

To serve, remove the thyme and parsley and discard. Toss the celery leaves with the lemon juice. Divide the stew evenly among warmed wide shallow bowls and top with the celery leaves. Serve right away.

Andrew Ticer (right) whisks roux while Michael Hudman prepares collards and neck bone gravy at their Memphis restaurant Hog & Hominy.

ROMAINE SALAD, PECORINO VINAIGRETTE & CHICKEN SKIN

Makes **4 servings**

FOR THE PECORINO VINAIGRETTE

- ¾ cup (6 fluid ounces/185 ml) heavy cream
- ¼ cup (2 fluid ounces/60 ml) whole milk
- ¼ cup (2 ounces/60 grams) good-quality, fresh ricotta cheese
- ½ cup (2 ounces/60 grams) grated pecorino romano cheese
- 2 tablespoons sherry vinegar
- 2 tablespoons red wine vinegar
- 2 teaspoons Roasted Garlic (recipe follows)
- Finely grated zest of 1 lemon
- ½ teaspoon dry mustard
- Kosher salt and freshly ground pepper

- Skin from 4 chicken breasts
- Canola oil for deep-frying
- Kosher salt and freshly ground pepper
- 1 head romaine lettuce
- Small block of Parmigiano-Reggiano cheese

Editor's Wine Choice Bright, crisp, pear-scented Sicilian white: 2012 Tasca Leone d'Almerita

Grabbing a quick lunch at Gus's Fried Chicken, our favorite local fried-chicken spot, inspired this salad, a play on a Caesar that uses our pecorino vinaigrette. As we were mowing through Gus's chicken, we agreed that the best part was the crispy skin, so we decided to add it to our salad in place of croutons. The dish quickly became a favorite at the restaurant. For a heartier dish, grill the chicken breasts from which the skin was removed, cut them into strips, and serve them with the salad. —*Michael*

To make the vinaigrette, in a large bowl, whisk together the cream, milk, ricotta, and pecorino cheese. Whisk in the sherry and wine vinegars, roasted garlic, lemon zest, mustard, salt to taste, and 1 teaspoon pepper. The consistency will be similar to a Caesar dressing. Refrigerate until ready to serve.

In a small saucepan, combine the chicken skin and ¼ cup (2 fluid ounces/60 ml) water, place over medium-low heat, and bring to a gentle simmer. What we are doing here is rendering the fat, which will take about 15 minutes. Once the fat has been rendered out of the skin, drain the skin. (If you like, reserve the rendered fat, which is also known as schmaltz. You can make amazing toast with it.) Flatten the chicken skins on a work surface and let them cool.

Pour canola oil into a deep-fryer to the fill line, or pour the oil to a depth of 2 inches (5 cm) into a deep, heavy sauté pan. Heat the oil to 375°F (190°C) on a deep-frying thermometer. Carefully add the cooled chicken skins to the hot oil and fry until golden brown, about 6 minutes. Transfer the fried skins to paper towels to drain and sprinkle with a pinch of salt.

Separate the lettuce leaves, tear into bite-size pieces, and add to a salad bowl. Season with salt and pepper to taste and pour in just enough of the vinaigrette to coat the lettuce lightly; reserve the remaining vinaigrette for another use. Toss the leaves well with the vinaigrette. You can use tongs, or just use your hands, which helps coat the salad evenly. (That's what Maw Maw did, anyway.)

continued on page 254

ROMAINE SALAD, PECORINO VINAIGRETTE & CHICKEN SKIN *continued*

Divide the dressed greens among individual plates. Break the chicken skins into small pieces and distribute evenly over the salads. Using a vegetable peeler, shave the Parmigiano-Reggiano over the salads and serve right away.

Roasted Garlic & Roasted Garlic Oil

Makes **about ½ cup (4 ounces/ 125 grams) roasted garlic and 2¾ cups (22 fluid ounces/650 ml) roasted garlic oil**

4 **heads garlic, cut in half crosswise**

3 **cups (24 fluid ounces/700 ml) extra-virgin olive oil**

Preheat the oven to 350°F (180°C). Put the garlic in a baking dish, cut side up, and pour the olive oil over the garlic. Cover the dish with aluminum foil and roast until the garlic is soft and golden brown, about 30 minutes.

Remove the garlic heads from the baking dish and set aside until cool enough to handle. Then squeeze the soft garlic from the skins, place in an airtight container, and refrigerate for up to 5 days.

Strain the roasted garlic oil through a fine-mesh sieve into a bottle or jar, cap tightly, and store in the refrigerator for up to 1 week.

RICOTTA INFORNATA WITH CARROT BRODO

Total **1 hr**
Serves **6 as a first course**

- 1 **pound fresh ricotta cheese**
- 1½ **pounds fresh fava beans, shelled**
- 1 **pound asparagus, tips left whole and stalks thinly sliced crosswise**
- 3 **tablespoons extra-virgin olive oil**
- 2 **tablespoons fresh lemon juice**

Kosher salt and pepper

- 1½ **cups fresh carrot juice**
- 2 **tablespoons sorghum molasses (see Note)**
- 2 **tablespoons fresh lime juice**
- ½ **teaspoon cayenne pepper**

A specialty of Sardinia and Sicily, *ricotta infornata* ("fired ricotta") features fresh ricotta cheese that's slow-baked until a speckled, charred crust surrounds the soft center. Ticer and Hudman add a Southern spin to their first-course version by serving the baked cheese in a bright carrot-citrus broth with sorghum and fava beans— their play on peas and carrots.

1. Preheat the oven to 500°F. On a large baking sheet lined with parchment paper, shape the ricotta into a 2-inch-thick round. Bake for about 30 minutes, until lightly browned. Let cool slightly, then cut into 12 wedges.

2. Meanwhile, fill a bowl with ice water. In a large saucepan of salted boiling water, blanch the fava beans until the skins just start to wrinkle, 1 to 2 minutes. Drain the favas and transfer them to the ice bath to cool. Drain again, then pinch them out of their skins.

3. Set up another ice bath. Fill the large saucepan with water, bring to a boil and add a generous pinch of salt. Blanch the asparagus and peeled favas until crisp-tender, about 1 minute. Using a slotted spoon, transfer to the ice bath to cool. Drain well and transfer to a medium bowl. Add 1 tablespoon each of the olive oil and lemon juice and season the salad with salt and pepper.

4. In a large bowl, whisk the carrot juice with the sorghum molasses, lime juice, cayenne and the remaining 2 tablespoons of olive oil and 1 tablespoon of lemon juice. Season the *brodo* with salt and pepper.

5. Ladle the *brodo* into 6 shallow bowls. Mound some of the asparagus and fava salad in the center of each and top with 2 wedges of *ricotta infornata*. Serve right away.

NOTE Sorghum molasses, sometimes called sorghum syrup, is available at grocery stores like Whole Foods and online at *zingermans.com.*

MAKE AHEAD The carrot *brodo* can be refrigerated overnight.

For more on Andrew Ticer & Michael Hudman
andrewmichaelitaliankitchen.com
Andrew Michael Italian Kitchen
@amitaliancooks

ONE-POT WONDERS

Cooking in One Pot, One Wok, One Casserole or One Skillet with 250 All-in-One Recipes

BY **CLIFFORD A. WRIGHT**

UNLIKE cookbook authors who promote the most obvious benefit of one-pot cooking–easy cleanup–Clifford A. Wright has a culinary reason for preferring it: He believes it is a fantastic way to build layer upon layer of flavor. For his meatball and yogurt chowder (page 261), he starts with chickpeas, then adds lentils, then meatballs, then spinach, then yogurt, and so on, building complexity in the dish. He takes a slightly different approach to his turkey vindaloo (page 260): Many of the ingredients are added at once, but the long, single-pot simmer gives the dish its boldly spiced sauce. And even though he doesn't trumpet it, it's still true: There's only one pot to wash when you're done.

Published by John Wiley & Sons, $24

PORTUGUESE KALE SOUP

Makes **8 servings**

- 2 tablespoons extra-virgin olive oil
- ½ cup diced salt pork
- 1 large onion, chopped
- 2 garlic cloves, crushed
- 2 pounds fingerling or red potatoes, cut into 1-inch cubes
- 1 pound ripe tomatoes, cut in half, seeds squeezed out, and grated against the largest holes of a grater
- 1 pound linguiça or kielbasa, cut up
- 1 pound kale, trimmed of heaviest stems and sliced
- 6 cups water
- 5 teaspoons salt
- 1 tablespoon dry white wine or sherry vinegar
- 1 teaspoon dried thyme
- 1 teaspoon freshly ground black pepper
- ¼ teaspoon red chile flakes

Pinch of saffron, crumbled (optional)

- 2 pounds striped bass, sea bass, or other firm-fleshed fish fillets, cut into large chunks
- 24 littleneck clams, washed well and soaked in cold water to cover for 30 minutes with 1 tablespoon baking soda, then drained

Editor's Beer Choice Nicely hoppy New England pale ale: Cisco Brewers Whale's Tale

Contrary to the name, this is actually a stew popular on Cape Cod and in southeastern Massachusetts and first made by Portuguese immigrants, who have a long, historic, and strong presence there. A good number of traditional, and old, Cape Cod dishes are called Portuguese-style, such as this luscious stew with fish, clams, linguiça sausage, and kale. Many of the local clam shacks on Cape Cod will offer a Portuguese kale soup or a variation on this recipe. The Portuguese-style linguiça sausage is rather easily found in supermarkets in New England, but elsewhere you can use Spanish-style (not Mexican-style) chorizo, hot Italian sausage, Cajun andouille sausage, or Polish kielbasa.

1. To a large soup pot or flameproof baking casserole over medium heat, add the olive oil and then the salt pork and cook, stirring occasionally, until crispy, about 10 minutes. Add the onion and garlic and cook, stirring, until softened, about 5 minutes. Add the potatoes, tomatoes, linguiça sausage, kale, water, salt, vinegar, thyme, pepper, red chile flakes, and saffron, if using, bring to a boil, then reduce the heat to low, cover, and simmer until the potatoes are nearly cooked, 40 to 45 minutes.

2. Turn the heat to high and bring to a furious boil. Add the fish and clams, and cook until the clams open, 8 to 10 minutes. Discard any clams that have not opened. Check the seasoning. Let sit for 5 to 10 minutes before serving.

TURKEY VINDALOO

Makes **4 servings**

- 1 tablespoon ground coriander
- 1 teaspoon ground turmeric
- 1 teaspoon ground cumin
- ½ teaspoon ground cloves
- 3 fresh green chiles
- One 1-inch piece ginger, peeled
- 4 large garlic cloves
- ½ cup white wine vinegar
- 3 tablespoons vegetable oil
- 2 large onions, cut in half, then thinly sliced
- 3 pounds turkey parts such as thigh, breast, wings, cut up into smaller serving pieces
- 3 Yukon Gold, white, or red potatoes (1¼ pounds), peeled and cut into ¾-inch cubes
- 1½ cups water
- 1 cinnamon stick
- 2 teaspoons salt
- 1 cup fresh or frozen peas

Editor's Wine Choice Fruity, full-bodied, off-dry German Riesling: 2011 Dönnhoff

This spicy-hot dish from Goa on India's west coast is typical fare in most Indian restaurants. In this recipe it's made with turkey rather than chicken and is served with warmed naan or other flatbread.

1. In a small bowl, mix the coriander, turmeric, cumin, and cloves together. In a blender, blend together the spice mixture, chiles, ginger, garlic, and vinegar until smooth.

2. In a large sauté pan, heat the oil over medium heat, then add the onions and cook, stirring, until golden, about 20 minutes. Add the turkey, potatoes, water, cinnamon stick, salt, and the vinegar mixture from the blender, cover, reduce the heat to low, and simmer, stirring occasionally, until the turkey and potatoes are tender, about 1 hour. Add the peas 5 minutes before the turkey is done. Remove and discard the cinnamon stick. Serve hot.

MEATBALL & YOGURT CHOWDER

Makes **4 servings**

5 cups water

One 15-ounce can chickpeas, rinsed and drained

¼ cup brown lentils

2½ teaspoons salt, or more as needed

1 teaspoon freshly ground black pepper, or more as needed

1 pound ground beef

1 medium onion, finely chopped

10 ounces baby spinach leaves

⅓ cup chopped fresh dill

3 cups whole-milk plain yogurt, whipped with a fork

This exceedingly simple preparation can be whipped up in about 30 minutes. It will surprise you because you'll think you're tasting far more spices and ingredients than are actually in the chowder. At the end you need to be careful that the yogurt doesn't cook too much, as it will curdle, so only keep it on the stovetop long enough to heat it, then serve immediately.

1. In a large saucepan, bring the water to a boil over high heat with the chickpeas. Add the lentils, 2 teaspoons of salt, and the pepper and boil, stirring occasionally, for 15 minutes.

2. Meanwhile, in a bowl, mix together the beef, onion, and remaining ½ teaspoon salt and form into walnut-size meatballs.

3. Reduce the heat to medium-low. Place the meatballs in the soup and stir to coat them. Cook the meatballs, turning occasionally, for 15 minutes.

4. Reduce the heat to low. Add the spinach and dill and cook, stirring and folding gently to immerse the leaves without breaking the meatballs, for another 5 minutes. Stir in the yogurt and cook only until it is heated through, about 2 minutes. Toss and correct the seasoning if necessary, then serve.

STIR-FRIED GREEN BEANS WITH GROUND PORK & SHRIMP

Makes **4 servings**

- 4 cups vegetable oil
- 3 pounds green beans, trimmed
- 2 large garlic cloves, finely chopped
- ¾ pound ground pork
- ½ pound medium shrimp (about 14), shelled and chopped
- ¼ cup chicken broth
- 1 tablespoon chile-garlic sauce
- ¼ cup water
- 1 tablespoon soy sauce
- 2 teaspoons salt
- 1½ teaspoons sugar
- 2 teaspoons rice vinegar
- 1 teaspoon sesame oil
- 2 scallions, trimmed and chopped

Editor's Wine Choice Minerally, vibrant Sauvignon Blanc: 2011 Le Domaine Saget Pouilly-Fumé

This is a wonderful recipe if you want to get more vegetables into your diet. It's mostly green beans flavored with pork and shrimp. Everything cooks fast and easy. The chile-garlic sauce is sold in jars in your supermarket's Asian food aisle. A common brand is one by Lee Kum Kee. Don't be tempted to cook all the green beans at once to speed things up, or your dinner will be greasy and unappetizing: You must cook them in batches.

1. In a wok, heat the vegetable oil over high heat until it starts to smoke, then cook the green beans in 4 batches until slightly crispy looking, 2 minutes per batch. Remove the green beans with a slotted spoon or skimmer and reserve on a paper towel–lined platter to drain. After every batch let the oil reheat for a minute before putting in the next batch. Carefully (because it's hot) pour off all but 4 tablespoons of oil. (You may want to wait until the oil has cooled a bit before pouring off. Let the oil cool completely and save for future frying if desired.)

2. Let the remaining oil heat over high heat, then add the garlic and cook, stirring, for 10 seconds. Add the pork, shrimp, broth, and chile-garlic sauce and cook, stir-frying, for 2 minutes. Add the water, soy sauce, salt, and sugar and toss for 30 seconds. Return all the green beans to the wok and cook, stir-frying, until the liquid has nearly evaporated, about 4 minutes. Stir in the rice vinegar, sesame oil, and scallions. Toss once or twice and serve.

POLLO 'NCIP 'NCIAP (CHICKEN BRAISED IN WINE WITH ROSEMARY)

Active **30 min;** Total **1 hr 30 min**
Serves **6**

- 4 tablespoons extra-virgin olive oil
- 2 large garlic cloves, crushed
- 1 medium onion, thinly sliced
- 1 Fresno chile or red jalapeño, seeded and chopped, or 1 dried árbol chile pepper, crumbled

One 4-pound chicken, cut into 8 pieces

Kosher salt and pepper

- 1 cup dry white wine
- 1 teaspoon finely chopped rosemary
- 1 cup chicken stock or low-sodium broth

Editor's Wine Choice
Citrusy, medium-bodied Italian white: 2012 Vinosia Falanghina

"This dish from the Marche region of Italy is a favorite with home cooks because it is quick to prep," says Wright. "In fact, *'ncip 'nciap* ("chop–chop") indicates something prepared rapidly."

1. In a large enameled cast-iron casserole, heat the oil. Add the garlic and onion and cook over moderately low heat, stirring occasionally, until softened and lightly golden, 8 to 10 minutes. Stir in the chile. Season the chicken with salt and pepper, add to the casserole and cook over moderate heat, turning, until golden all over, 6 to 7 minutes. Stir in the wine.

2. Cover the casserole and cook over low heat for 30 minutes, turning the chicken halfway through. Add the rosemary and stock and bring to a boil; cover and cook over low heat for 15 minutes. Uncover and cook until the chicken is cooked through and the sauce has thickened, about 15 minutes longer.

3. Transfer the chicken to a serving platter. Season the sauce with salt and pepper and spoon over the chicken. Serve warm.

For more on Clifford A. Wright
cliffordawright.com
Clifford A. Wright
@CliffordAWright

INDEX

Page numbers in **bold** indicate photographs.

CREDITS

THE GRAMERCY TAVERN COOKBOOK
Book Cover, copyright © 2013 by Random House LLC; "Flounder with Marinated Cucumbers and Yogurt Sauce," "Baked Clams," and "Chocolate Bread Pudding" from *The Gramercy Tavern Cookbook* by Michael Anthony, produced by Dorothy Kalins, with a History by Danny Meyer, copyright © 2013 by Gramercy Tavern Corp. Used by permission of Clarkson Potter/ Publishers, an imprint of the Crown Publishing Group, a division of Random House LLC. All rights reserved. Photographs copyright © 2013 by Maura McEvoy.

ANNIE BELL'S BAKING BIBLE
From *Annie Bell's Baking Bible* by Annie Bell. Text © Annie Bell 2012. Photographs © Con Poulos 2012. Used by permission of Kyle Books.

CARAMEL
Photographs by Alexandra DeFurio from *Caramel* by Carole Bloom, reprinted with permission by Gibbs Smith.

KEEPERS
From *Keepers: Two Home Cooks Share Their Tried-and-True Weeknight Recipes and the Secrets to Happiness in the Kitchen* by Kathy Brennan and Caroline Campion. Copyright © 2013 by Kathy Brennan and Caroline Campion. Photographs by Christopher Testani. Used by permission of Rodale.

FLOUR, TOO
From *Flour, Too* © 2013 by Joanne Chang; photographs by Michael Harlan Turkell. Used with permission of Chronicle Books, LLC, San Francisco. Visit ChronicleBooks.com.

THE CHEFS COLLABORATIVE COOKBOOK
From *The Chefs Collaborative Cookbook* by Chefs Collaborative and Ellen Jackson. Photography by Gentl & Hyers. Published by The Taunton Press in 2013.

L.A. SON
Four recipes with interior photos, author photo, book cover from *L.A. Son* by Roy Choi with Tien Nguyen and Natasha Phan. Photographs by Bobby Fisher. Copyright © 2013 by Roy Choi, Tien Nguyen, and Natasha Phan. Reprinted by permission of HarperCollins Publishers.

ROOT-TO-STALK COOKING
Photographs, by Clay McLachlan, copyright © 2013 by Clay McLachlan; Book Cover, copyright © 2013 by Random House LLC; "Prep Tip for Shaved Broccoli Stalk Salad with Lime & Cotija," "Beet Greens Strata," "Fennel-Braised Pork Roast," and "Shaved Broccoli Stalk Salad with Lime & Cotija" from *Root-to-Stalk Cooking: The Art of Using the Whole Vegetable* by Tara Duggan, text copyright © 2013 by Tara Duggan. Used by permission of Ten Speed Press, an imprint of the Crown Publishing Group, a division of Random House LLC. All rights reserved.

RIVER COTTAGE VEG
Book Cover, copyright © 2011 by Random House LLC; "Warm Salad of Mushrooms and Roasted Squash," "Pistachio Dukka," and "Leeks (and Greens) with Coconut Milk" from *River Cottage Veg: 200 Inspired Vegetable Recipes* by Hugh Fearnley-Whittingstall, text copyright © 2011 by Hugh Fearnley-Whittingstall. Used by permission of Ten Speed Press, an imprint of the Crown Publishing Group, a division of Random House LLC. All rights reserved. Photographs copyright © 2011 by Simon Wheeler.

FRANNY'S
Excerpted from *Franny's*. Copyright © 2013 by Andrew Feinberg, Francine Stephens and Melissa Clark. Used by permission of Artisan, a division of Workman Publishing Co., Inc., New York. All rights reserved. Photographs copyright © 2013 by John von Pamer.

SWEET
Excerpted from *Sweet*. Copyright © 2013 by Valerie Gordon. Used by permission of Artisan, a division of Workman Publishing Co., Inc., New York. All rights reserved. Photographs copyright © 2013 by Peden + Munk.

I LOVE NEW YORK
Book Cover, copyright © 2013 by Random House LLC; "Delmonico Steak," "Lamb Rack with Cucumber Yogurt," and "Mashed Zucchini with Mint" from *I Love New York: Ingredients and Recipes* by Daniel Humm and Will Guidara, copyright © 2013 by Made Nice, LLC. Used by permission of Ten Speed Press, an imprint of the Crown Publishing Group, a division of Random House LLC. All rights reserved. Photographs copyright © 2013 by Francesco Tonelli.

SMOKE & PICKLES
Excerpted from *Smoke & Pickles*. Copyright © 2013 by Edward Lee. Used by permission of Artisan, a division of Workman Publishing Co., Inc., New York. All rights reserved. Photographs copyright © 2013 by Grant Cornett.

EXOTIC TABLE
Excerpted from *Exotic Table: Flavors, Inspiration, and Recipes from Around the World–to Your Kitchen*. Copyright

FOOD&**WINE**
BOOKS

More books from
FOOD&WINE

Annual Cookbook
More than 700 recipes from the world's best cooks, including
culinary legends Paula Wolfert and Jacques Pépin and star
chefs like Thomas Keller, Jamie Oliver and Nancy Silverton.

Cocktails
Over 150 of the decade's best drink recipes and favorite
party food from acclaimed mixologists and chefs. Plus
an indispensable guide to cocktail basics and the top bars
and lounges around the country.

Wine Guide
An essential, pocket-size guide focusing on the most reliable
producers, with over 1,000 stellar wines.